# The Digital Evangelist

# The House of Prisca and Aquila

Our mission at the House of Prisca and Aquila is to produce quality books that expound accurately the word of God to empower women and men to minister together in a multicultural church. Our writers have a positive view of the Bible as God's revelation that affects both thoughts and words, so it is plenary, historically accurate, and consistent in itself, fully reliable, and authoritative as God's revelation. Because God is true, God's revelation is true, inclusive to men and women, and speaking to a multicultural church, wherein all the diversity of the church is represented within the parameters of egalitarianism and inerrancy.

The word of God is what we are expounding, thereby empowering women and men to minister together in all levels of the church and home. The reason we say women and men together is because that is the model of Prisca and Aquila, ministering together to another member of the church—Apollos: "Having heard Apollos, Priscilla and Aquila took him aside and more accurately expounded to him the Way of God" (Acts 18:26). True exposition, like true religion, is by no means boring—it is fascinating. Books that reveal and expound God's true nature "burn within us" as they elucidate the Scripture and apply it to our lives.

This was the experience of the disciples who heard Jesus on the road to Emmaus: "Were not our hearts burning while Jesus was talking to us on the road, while he was opening the scriptures to us?" (Luke 24:32). We are hoping to create the classics of tomorrow, significant and accessible trade and academic books that "burn within us."

Our "house" is like the home to which Prisca and Aquila no doubt brought Apollos as they took him aside. It is like the home in Emmaus where Jesus stopped to break bread and reveal his presence. It is like the house built on the rock of obedience to Jesus (Matt 7:24). Our "house," as a euphemism for our publishing team, is a home where truth is shared and Jesus' Spirit breaks bread with us, nourishing all of us with his bounty of truth.

We are delighted to work together with Wipf and Stock in this series and welcome submissions on a wide variety of topics from an egalitarian, inerrantist global perspective.

For more information, see our website:

https://sites.google.com/site/houseofpriscaandaquila/.

# The Digital Evangelist

*Expanding Your Ministry by Writing for Publication*

EDITED BY

JEANNE C. DEFAZIO

AND

WILLIAM DAVID SPENCER

WIPF & STOCK · Eugene, Oregon

THE DIGITAL EVANGELIST
Expanding Your Ministry by Writing for Publication

The House of Prisca and Aquila



Wipf & Stock
An Imprint of Wipf and Stock Publishers
199 W. 8th Ave., Suite 3
Eugene, OR 97401

www.wipfandstock.com

PAPERBACK ISBN: 979-8-3852-6021-8
HARDCOVER ISBN: 979-8-3852-6022-5
EBOOK ISBN: 979-8-3852-6023-2

VERSION NUMBER 041026

This book is dedicated to Mel Novak.
Thanks for letting us see God in you, Mel.

# Contents

# Dedication

## Jeanne DeFazio

"Christianity, standing as one of the world's most prominent religions, has not escaped the transformative reach of social media platforms."[1]

Christians connect via Facebook, Instagram, X, and TikTok. Zoom and YouTube have expanded the global digital congregation. The iconic American-born Pope Leo XIV leads prayer via YouTube and multitudes subscribe. Since the pandemic, the postmodern Christian worships, prays, studies the Bible, and takes communion via Zoom uploaded to YouTube. Technology has connected the church despite geographical boundaries. Believers in Pakistan view Gemma Wenger's weekly church services via social media from her Bel Air living room.

This book includes testimonies from high profile Christians who have expanded their ministry publishing the gospel in blogs, articles, and books on and offline. These postmodern Christians preach God's word on social media platforms. For those who have gone viral for the Lord—well done, good and faithful servants. Thanks for pioneering and modeling millennial evangelism for the future of the church and sharing your stories with us.

1. A., "Influence of Social Media," para. 2.

# Acknowledgments

## Jeanne's Acknowledgments

Special thanks to Reverend Dr. Aída Besançon Spencer for graciously contributing her expertise in editing the earliest and roughest version of this manuscript. I'm really grateful to Mayor Bapu Vaitla for all he has done to feed the poor. I'm so happy that Pope Leo XIV became the first American pope. I am indebted to Pastor Darin Poullard and the wonderful congregation at Fort Washington Baptist Church for their generosity. I appreciate Pastor Dan Snape at the Community Congregational Church for his feedback. Thanks to Burke Fong for participating in the Digital Evangelist seminar and for supporting this book. Thanks to the Washington National Cathedral for posting services on YouTube. Thanks to Dr. Koen Van Rompay for live streaming his Sahaya International events. I'm grateful to Dr. Robb Davis for a lifetime of devotion to those in need. Thanks to Leslie McKinney Attema for her prayer support. Thanks to Zena Lane who helped me pick out new shoes. Thanks to Pastors Jaymz and Pascale Sideras of Revive Boston for including me in their Monday night Zoom prayer meeting. I truly appreciate Bishop Joseph and Reverend Katherine Kalema for expanding their ministry on social media. Gratitude to Grace May and Jasmin Sung for helping me when I needed it. I so appreciate Andrea Van Boven for her help. I am so proud of my awesome niece, Ella Louise Ryan, a recent graduate of UC San Diego with a bachelor of science degree in biological sciences. I am grateful to Rose Redington for being a wonderful friend. God bless Mary Ciarcia for her prayer support. Thanks to Patty Alfeld for her kindness and hospitality, and thanks to her wonderful friend Houghton Brown for being such a blessing. I'm especially grateful to the International Church of God in Burlington for all their support. I'm forever grateful to my friend Charlene Eber for encouraging me. Thank you to Rabbi Jim Morgan for welcoming me to the online Shabbat services of the Worship and Study Minyan at Harvard Hillel. Many thanks to Governor Jerry Brown, Senator Jay Rockefeller, and Peter Lynch for their support of this book. Thanks to the late Michael P. Grace II for the opportunity to coordinate his Christian outreaches. Many thanks to Caleb and Bonny Loring for advancing the kingdom of God. Thank you, Jesus, for giving me the strength to keep going.

## Bill's Acknowledgments

Aída, always, for all her gracious love and kindness, and all of our readers past and present. I hope this book will help all of you with your goals to serve our wonderful Lord and Savior, Jesus Christ, following the guidance of the Holy Spirit to the glory of the Father: one loving God in three co-eternal and co-equal Persons, the true and only God.

# PART ONE

# The Steps To Take To Become A Publishing Evangelist

William David Spencer

# Chapter One

# Expanding Your Ministry by Writing for Publication

**William David Spencer**

In this chapter, I will be sharing advice on how to prepare to write for publication.

I will also give you nine writing hints to equip your work for getting a hearing.

I will provide a questionnaire for you to use in editing short pieces.

And I will share some strategies on how to start, if your goal is publishing.

My goal is that this information enriches your manuscripts (or, more probably, typescripts) and helps you get them together to be viewed by an acquisitions editor. And to illustrate these points, I will tell you how I received my start in publishing articles, poems, other short pieces, and, finally, books. I will also begin and conclude with a mission statement I believe all Christian writers should follow. So, let's start.

## Preparing to Write for Publication

To begin, count the cost! On the rare occasions when anybody asks me what the life of a writer is like, I always advise them, "Only write if you cannot NOT write." If we are doers who are out and about, constantly making things happen, changing the world, performing courageous actions down to the last shovel-full of strenuous work, we're probably not going to be the people to write about it. The woman or man who interviews us and takes that recording home to spend hours transcribing it in detail to capture just what readers need to know about our inspiring life may be a very different kind of person than we worker bees are. Our biographer, the writer, or, perhaps, ghost writer has been gifted by the Holy Spirit to fulfill a calling that demands a lot of attention to detail and hours in front of the computer to shape our story into something connected and coherent that will sweep readers into our active world.

Therefore, the first step in any would-be writer's life is prayer: getting on our knees humbly before God and asking if this is really what God has gifted us to do. And we should keep praying every day, while we are writing anything, and whenever we have a problem in the process of writing. This is what I do: soak everything in prayer.

Next, let's anchor on a definition of what it means to publish, so that we're not just drifting about in a sea of confusion but we understand clearly what our task is. If we want to put this in writing terms, we could use this metaphor: we need to make sure we're all on the same page.[1]

According to *Webster's Unabridged Dictionary*, the term "publication" means "1. the act of publishing a book, periodical, map, piece of music, engraving or the like; 2. the act of bringing [it] before the public."[2]

Do you see how flexible the term "publication" is? It encompasses numerous works authors present publicly. Today, we would add e-mails, e-articles, and e-books.

In the ancient days, authors would read their manuscripts publicly and customers would hire scribes to write down their words, or students would sit at their professors' feet and scratch out notes, assembling textbooks for their studies, or their libraries, or their own future teaching.

We, however, are not living in those days, or even in more recent ones, when families relaxed together around the fire and read the latest installment of Charles Dickens's current saga. Since then, books particularly have taken it on the chin from radio, then television, then movies.

Today, with personal computers, iPads, and the internet, we are bombarded with sounds and visuals from early in our lives, through video games, news reports (broadcasting events even as they take place), music videos, and scads of information steeped in a metaverse of opinions, some by other humans and some by artificial intelligence, repeatedly assaulting us with data. And all of this clamor is engulfed in a tsunami of advertisements, inundating everyone who ventures out on the stormy sea of websites.

1. The Stack Exchange website traces the use of the phrase "on the same page" to *The New York Times*, Jan. 18, 1979, discussing an agreement on football rules: Stack Exchange, "What's the Origin," para. 7.

2. *Webster's Unabridged Dictionary*, "Publication," 1563.

E-books have tried to ease the impact, but sales are down for magazines and newspapers and all types of books.

Acquisitions editors at publishing businesses are responsible to sort through submissions of prospective books, articles, stories, poems, choosing to select, secure, and present for print to their editorial teams what they consider to be the best writing projects that their readers' demographic studies suggest have the most potential to sell. Those are the ones they will prepare with prospective authors to submit for consideration. Every submission not selected will usually be rejected.

So, how does any would-be author shoulder her or his way into this industry?

## Here Are Nine Writing Hints to Equip Your Work to Gain a Hearing

If you see writing as a ministry, then it is both about expressing your views in a way people will want to read and, at the same time, need to read, as you are guided by the Holy Spirit. Your mission statement, then, is to please God and edify your audience.

Therefore, make your work accessible. Today, shorter sentences are more accessible. In Bible times, people's attention spans seem to have been longer, since the apostle Paul could write long sentences with many parts. Now, according to Steph Jackman of International Accreditors for Continuing Education and Training (IACET), the global, non-profit standards-setting organization for education and training programs, "Research shows humans have an 8.25-second attention span and prefer short content. Interestingly, when viewing a video, our attention span increases significantly from 8.25 seconds to 120 seconds."[3] (Are you all still with me? What were we talking about? Hmm . . . I paused to watch a crazy cat video.)[4]

People often ask me why I use no cell phone. As a writer and a professor, I need time for sustained thought. I can't really keep up with e-mail, as it is. If I'm being texted constantly, flooded with more advertisements, getting updates, and on and on, all concentrated thought will evaporate.

3. Jackman, "Short Attention Spans," para. 11.

4. This whimsical reference is to an hilarious illustration of a short attention span getting swept away in the midst of mounting action in one of my wife's and my favorite movies: *Dancer and the Dame*, www.PureFlix.com/DancerAndTheDame.

Recently, we invited some college students over for a meal after church to get to know them. As soon as they arrived, they all pulled out their cell phones and started in. We asked a few questions about them. In a brief pause, two of them offered brief answers, pleasantly enough, then dove right back with the others into their phones. So, we sat with them in silence. Our son, who works at a public access cable station, told us he had the same experience teaching a class on producing videos for a nearby college. He advised us, "It's a good thing you didn't complain. They might have immediately texted it to all their friends on Instagram."

The lesson from all of this? Write short sentences! I'm not particularly writing long hypotactic sentences in this chapter, but I'm not writing short paratactic sentences either. Why not? Because, if I've lost you, then you are probably not being called to be a writer because you haven't scraped together enough time or sustained thought to write!

Having said that, I still believe writing short, brief but poignant sentences that will move readers along is worthwhile. Don't bog them down in a lot of verbosity.

Use strong verbs. Don't overuse "is." Especially try to avoid "is" in constructions like this one: it is very important not to overuse the verb "is"! What is very important?! Who knows? Nobody knows! The referent here is vague. Write, instead: very important is not to overuse the verb "is"! That is so much clearer. We face the same problem with "there are" constructions, as in, "There are many people who avoid eating gluten." "Many people exist who avoid eating gluten" is clearer.

If you are creating fiction, not overusing "is" becomes essential. For example, don't write, "Emily is in the doorway." Use your verbs and adverbs to give your reader a feeling for what kind of person your character Emily is. Does she stalk into a room? Flounce in? Creep in? Burst in? Sidle in? Stand in the doorway, seething, chuckling, or shaking with fury or terror? Does she simply stick her head in and sweep the room with a commanding, diffident, sly, or charitable glance?

Here's an example of a very simple transitional pair of sentences I used to move readers swiftly from one encounter to another in *Cave of Little Faces*, a novel my wife and I enjoyed writing together.

*Cave of Little Faces*

I didn't want to belabor the transition and lose readers or distract them. At the same time, I wanted to give my readers a feeling for a new character we had introduced, Tomás, a volatile, pushy individual who was making demands on another character, Ricky, to take hasty action to solve a dilemma on the border of Haiti, as Tomás himself was already doing. Our readers had just faced an intense encounter between Ricky and Josefina, our protagonist, and Ricky's potential boss, whom he currently dislikes immensely. When Ricky hears a solid knock on his door, he assumes Jo is back for a last word. Hard knocking on doors is not reserved for men. As we all know from experience, capable women can be no-nonsense when they decide to get a job done. Ricky, whose consciousness is just beginning to be raised to this fact, is annoyed. So, how do I have Ricky open the door to describe his current mood? And how, instead, does Tomás enter? Does he explode in? Maybe, but that might be overkill, since he's been up all night. But, tired or not, he's still pushy. So, I wrote,

> Before [Ricky] could do anything, he was called back by another knock on his door. He frowned and tossed it open, assuming she was back again for something or other. Instead, his childhood friend Tomás, short, square, solid, pushed past him into the house. "What have you got to eat?" demanded Tomás. "I'm starving."

In this opening paragraph of chapter 21 on page 146 I used the verb "tossed" for the way Ricky opens his door, "pushed past him" for his friend's entry, and "demanded" for his friend's opening words. In this way, I have the verbs color the new scene for my readers. This is just one simple illustration of how verbs can bring your work alive and keep your readers' interest.

Use colorful, fresh illustrations and analogies. In my introduction for the chapter you're now reading, I intentionally used a cliché, "make sure we're all on the same page," as a little writing joke to lighten the tone of all this information I'm presently dumping on you. If I wanted to keep my metaphor consistent. I could have written a fresher phrase like "let's all set sail together," since I was using sea-faring imagery as an analogy. The choice depends on the kind of effect we want to make on our readers.

Normally, what is best is to avoid clichés (common, overused words or phrases, like "all on the same page"), unless we are intending to make our present character or passage prosaic. Sometimes, clichés do provide a familiar island of rest for readers to make them momentarily feel comfortable and safe. But, I realize, using one, of course, is always a dangerous thing to do. We have to let our readers know our book is not going to be a monotony of clichés, so we have to use them carefully. If we put one in our text, we should only do so for a very good reason. I once added a cliché ("creeping like a nun") into a poem to underscore the prosaic monotony of a chronic illness. I also used a different cliché intentionally once in a song lyric. I'm not sure, to this day, if either was a good idea. With fresh illustrations or turns of phrase, we usually can't go wrong, although I once read a book crammed with so many fresh turns of phrase, they got really tiresome. As the action submerged into the writer's styling, this reader was drowned.[5]

How much should we quote another person's writing? Jeanette Gardner Littleton cautions as little as possible. If a book is short, we should

5. For examples, see Rogers, *Dictionary of Clichés*.

be very brief. If it's long, the usual limit is three hundred to five hundred words. What we are striving for is called "fair usage."[6] Copyrighted material is a sensitive area in which to trespass. Best to write for permission than to face the legal shotgun for poaching in someone else's terrain. Even a hint of an accusation of plagiarism races around the industry, and we could be blacklisted from publishing. This happened to an award-winning columnist in our area. A critic discovered a similar piece from years before by someone else in a completely different publication that matched this columnist's latest entry. His publisher and readers were scandalized. As famous as he was as a journalist and, despite an instant apology and plea for forgiveness, he literally disappeared from print overnight, and I've never seen anything from him again. No reputable publisher wants a lawsuit.

If you are still determined to write a book, here's how we've found a handy way to build our books. My father was a painting contractor and mineralogist who loved books and filled every room with them. His knowledge was prodigious. Although he was not Hebrew in background, apparently, he shared the belief with his Jewish friends that all boys should be taught a trade. He chose his father's business, professional painting, since he detested having a boss and could only work happily if he himself was in charge. One summer day, while we were on the job, he asked me, "How would you price this house?" I was stymied. He said, "Well, how long would it take us to paint this side?" "Two days?" I offered. "Right!" he replied and then added, "Multiply that by four sides. And I work about twice as fast as you do, so I earn twice as much." That made sense to me. I was slow and meticulous, so he put me on the high job, the kid three stories up, painting the lattice work under the roof. Next, he asked, "How much does the paint cost?" Then he put it all together and we had our price.

When we had worked our way up to writing books, I and my wife adapted my dad's advice to our task. We asked our publishers how long each book should be, divided that length up into chapters (usually about fifteen to twenty pages each, double-spaced in size 12 font). Then we figured in approximately ten pages for the introduction (which is often written last, when the book is basically finished, since we now know for sure what's going to be in it) and ten pages for the conclusion: voilá! We had our basic structure. Now, we just had to paint it in, so as to say. The final task, of course, is to keep the filling inside the page limits because if we don't, the

6. See Littleton, "How Much Can I Quote?," 8.

publisher's editors will do that, and seeing those slash-outs they make on the pages (or in the columns beside them) is excruciating.

Writers often work alone. But being published is a joint effort that requires writers to adopt an attitude of teamwork. We have to be a reliable investment ourselves to produce a reliable product. In the ten years I edited *Priscilla Papers*, the journal for Christians for Biblical Equality International, and the seventeen years my wife and I have been editing *Africanus Journal*, what is astonishing to us is how many Christians, professors, and students volunteer to review a book, receive the book, and never produce a book review. They keep the book and don't send it back, but, despite the guidelines we provide for how to do their review and the reminders our staff sends out to them, they appear to have wandered off into the wasteland of No Reply, never to be heard from again.

An even more curious dead-end is when we send back grammatical corrections and questions for adding or improving a submission and nothing is ever returned. It's not like anyone yells at these remiss individuals. One gentleman died, so he had an excuse, but everyone else looks hail and hardy, yet, just doesn't get around to the revision. Do they pray for God's empowerment and guidance to bring their work into completion? The prayer for wisdom is one we notice God always answers. When it comes to reneging on finishing a book (as several prospective authors we know have done), the consequences are serious. Some publishers demand advances be paid back. Some authors whom publishers find difficult to work with are labeled "problem authors" and the opportunity to do another book evaporates.

What authors have to realize is that publishers are responsible to their employees, their editors, copy editors, acquisitions editors, their art department, those who work with the printers to keep on deadline, those who market, promote, create their publicity, their catalogs, their advertisements, and on and on. They and their families have to eat and pay their bills and heat their homes. Our books need to feed them all. This is why we all have to write books that people will want to read. This is why we learn to write like that in our church newsletter, our blog, our internet posts. We need to find out how to do a magazine article or a news item or a book so that it will enhance someone else's life and will please God by edifying our readers. We all need to write something that not only tells our readers what they need to know but attracts them by our style, so they will want to know. The best books focus their winsome style and fascinating data on leading readers to one main point. In our books like *Christian Egalitarian Leadership*, for example, our main guiding focus was to empower 100 percent of the church to use the gifts the Holy Spirit has given each believer to assist God in bringing in God's reign. Staying on that focus point leads to the next piece of advice.

We should not be afraid to eliminate words, sentences, even paragraphs that might distract, or even derail, readers from following the flow of our narrative (if we are writing fiction, or our argument if we are writing non-fiction). If we shake the boat with too many words, readers might fall out and swim for shore. Once a reader sets down your book in distraction (or we could say "bails out" if we want to keep our aquatic metaphor afloat), she or he is gone. Better we keep them up all night turning pages until their bleary-eyed morning dawns because, once they rest up and stop hating us for wrecking their night's sleep, they'll be back, craving to embark on our next book.

One more point to consider is to keep our international readers in mind as we write. Defining unusual terms is a good idea, especially for all readers unfamiliar with your field. Also, the latest practice of using "they" instead of "his" or "her" or "she" or "him" for a single referent creates what used to be called "numbers error" or "numbers fault." Mixing in plurals and singulars for the same referent can easily confuse those for whom English is already difficult to read. Keeping our referents clear helps readers who are English Language Learners (ELL) to keep plowing through our text.[7]

Make sure what we're working on has a main point or a thesis, an interesting start, a body, and, at the end, a summary of what we have written. Also, include at least one application in a short piece and more for a large piece.

My wife, a prolific, successful, and award-winning author who is working on her twenty-first book, and I created the following questionnaire to guide you in checking your writing. It deals with style of writing, content, and mechanics of writing. If you study this chart carefully before you write, then use it as your guide while you are writing, and, finally, check your written work with its questions, you will find it will improve your work and make what you produce more thorough.

7. For more information on this important issue of reaching out to a global world, please see a previous book Jeanne DeFazio and I edited, *Empowering English Language Learners: Successful Strategies of Christian Educators.*

## Editing for Short Pieces

Title ______________________ To:__________________________

Your name above.

From: Your email:

The following items are rated according to the following symbols:

I = inadequate; A = adequate; G = good; S = superior

### STYLE OF WRITING

Are the sentences clear, accessible, succinct? ................ I A G S

Are illustrations and analogies used? ...................... I A G S

Is the writing fresh, free from clichés, colorful, winsome? .... I A G S

Are strong verbs used? ................................ I A G S

Is the data fascinating? ................................ I A G S

Are quotations brief and relevant to the flow
of the argument? ...................................... I A G S

### CONTENT

Is the content pleasing to God? .......................... I A G S

Does the content have some biblical basis? ................. I A G S

Is the piece real? ...................................... I A G S

Does the author show familiarity with the content? .......... I A G S

Is it well-organized? .................................. I A G S

Does it have a thesis or main point,
introductory paragraph or sentence,
body,
and summary?

Does the argument or thought flow logically?
Is it purposeful? ...................................... I A G S

Is at least one application included that flows
from the body? ....................................... I A G S

Are the conclusions proved by supporting data
and explanations? ..................................... I A G S

Is the idea or presentation original or unique? .............. I A G S

Does the content relate to a specific audience? .............. I A G S

Are helpful insights presented? .......................... I A G S

Does it have no extraneous materials or asides? ............. I A G S

## MECHANICS OF WRITING

Is the material accurate? ................................ I A G S

Are ideas of others footnoted? ........................... I A G S

Are Bible versions identified in parenthesis? ............... I A G S

Is a consistent and correct form used in footnotes? .......... I A G S

Are quotations and data double-checked? .................. I A G S

Is the piece the correct length for its objectives? ............ I A G S

Are spelling and grammar correct and consistent? ........... I A G S

Final comment: ___________



## So, How Do You Break Into the Industry? If Your Goal Is Publishing, Here's How to Start

1. Begin by setting your goals. Where do you want to focus? As we can see by Webster's wide definition, publishing can cover a vast area of products. Books, of course, get the most press for readers, but they are just one part of writing.

Some writers, of course, don't seek to be published at all. Emily Dickinson, who wrote close to 1,800 poems, had only 11 printed in her lifetime, and these might have been without her permission.[8] The main thing writers do is write all the time, because so many of us just enjoy creating with words. When you can please God and edify others, it's a ministry. Some of what we write gets published. A lot of it doesn't.

But it's still all about recording thoughts on paper, or on e-copy, and doing that creatively. So, books are just a sustained hyper-spacing of a daily activity.

8. Holton, "I Had Told You," para. 1.

Don't let the thought of writing scare you or threaten you and block you from writing. Writing is as natural as jotting a note down for your kids or your friends. It is an everyday part of life. It's simply saying things from your head with your hands, or recording them and employing another means to get thoughts into legible words besides saying them with your mouth.

One heroic example of a writer who could not *not* write was Jean-Dominique Bauby, a magazine editor who was sidelined by a stroke at age forty-five. *Los Angeles Times* journalist John-Thor Dahlburg reports, "Lying paralyzed on his hospital bed, he dictated by blinking his left eyelid, his only means of communication." His resultant book, *The Diving Suit and the Butterfly*, amazed France and was translated into English and other languages.[9] In the face of heroism and perseverance like this, we should all take heart and shoulder our way through timidity, kicking writer's block out of our way.

2. When writing for an audience to read, start sensibly in gaining experience by building a publishing track record. Unpublished writers should certainly begin with seeking opportunities to get published, but don't try to start with a book. That's like jumping cold into a cage with one of those mixed martial arts champions. You'll either run out of energy in five minutes, or in five pages, or, if you do manage to finish something sizable, editors will pound on your ego by rejecting your work with a form letter.

Instead, start with small pieces and build a track record that trains you. Publishers respect a list of your pile of published work that you've amassed with your own efforts. That is your best assurance to them that, if they give you a chance, you will come through.

3. So, start small—begin building your publishing resumé by seeking to publish in venues available to you. Opportunities are all around you, like church or business or other organizational newsletters. If you still have any local newspapers, study what they are printing—what they care about—and dive in by sending interesting letters to the editor. If your letter is published, find an appropriate topic to offer to do as a one-off guest column.

My first published pieces, done for a ninth-grade journalism class, were sent to the local newspaper. I reported school events. I also submitted a poem or story to my public high school's own student newspaper and its yearly literary journal. These set up a defining experience that came when

9. Dahlburg, "Stricken Man's Tale of Triumph," A16.

my excellent wrestling coach, who was also my excellent English teacher, Dr. Tom Grifa, seeing my interest in writing, convinced me to try for a VFW writing contest and I won. Our school's football queen, a senior and a fine writer herself, came in second and was so gracious to me, praising my article. The award was a $25 savings bond. What an experience that was for a little ninth grader! I wasn't paid again for anything I wrote until years later, when our band earned some money playing our original songs, but this VFW contest confirmed for me that I could write. I also learned that staying on the track is worthwhile because we never know when we'll surprise ourselves and win the garland.'

4. Today, a blog can be a door in—in fact, a blog post, in my experience, is one of the best avenues available for building a readership. We had no idea our monthly blog would ever reach 145,000 hits and still be growing rapidly. My wife and I were astonished. While I was just beginning to draft this chapter on writing, we discovered our blog had a tracking device that told us that very week, our blog's main activity was garnering a thousand hits from Brazil. Why Brazil??? Sure, I've always loved Brazilian music and, since I was a teenager, have been collecting Brazilian records and compact discs. We have wonderful Brazilian friends and love Guaraná, that fabulous Brazilian soda made from the fruit of the same name. Here in our Gordon-Conwell Theological Seminary's Boston Campus for Urban Ministerial Education, my wife, who is a senior professor of New Testament, and I, a biblical theologian, have been privileged to teach so many delightful and brilliant Brazilian students (a few of whom have tried to slip their term papers by us in Portuguese, figuring, since she can speak Spanish and I can speak some, we can navigate grading Portuguese, too, but they were all disappointed. These languages are too different). We haven't yet enjoyed a visit to beautiful Brazil itself. So, we're shocked and grateful so many Brazilians like our blog this much. Who knew?

Second, that same week were hits on our blog from the Netherlands. My wife has Dutch heritage; I've lectured as a guest ethicist at a robotics conference at the University of Leiden, and we've explored that amazing country, but we are overwhelmed by such kind attention. Our third mass of readers were from Vietnam, where we don't know of a previous connection at all. Fourth was Russia—wow! This is really humbling—that people all over the world find our blog posts useful. Back at home that month, the USA readers were down the list at number five.

The next month, the Netherlanders were number one, the Russians were number two, the USA readers were number three, the Brazilians were clocking in at number four. This month, the USA is on top at number one. In short, we never know until each month who our readers actually are. The nationalities vary in number (hopefully, they're not all bots, harvesting our information).

The same fact is true for *Africanus Journal*, which my wife and I founded and named for the great early church scholar Julius Africanus. For seventeen years, the journal has been produced in partnership with Gordon-Conwell's Boston campus. We know from emails to us and submissions of articles from African, Korean, Chinese, British, Filipino, and many other international scholars that our journal issues are being read all over the world. Why is that?

Along with enlightenment and guidance by the Holy Spirit, the secret, I think, why our blog posts and journal articles are being read so widely is that we and our many contributors, which include Gordon-Conwell faculty and students, as well as many other Christian thinkers all over the world, try to write interesting pieces about what each contributor cares about.

In other words, we don't tell our potential readers about what we had for breakfast. Who cares? Why would anybody read that? I wouldn't. Writing and publishing about something interesting that matters to us appeals to readers who care about that issue, too. Blogs cost little to create and maintain and, if each post is edifying and has a worthwhile topic that matters to God and people, such aspects are what are important to the readers we attract. Doing blogs also helps us stay on our mission to please God and edify readers. Blog entries can do a lot of good for God's kingdom in the world.

What is our approach? We call our blog *Applying Biblical Truths Today*.[10] We and our guest writers relate each blog posting to a Bible verse and blend in the relevance with some interesting report, fact, incident, issue, or story that captures our attention and seems to do the same with our readers.

5. Craft everything you write. Other ways to break into writing can begin as simply as correcting our emails, or even writing our own greeting cards (which I do when I can't find any I like). Make sure you double check everything you write. Don't email a reply so full of errors and omissions that

10. We warmly welcome everyone who is interested to find our blog by punching aandwspencer.blogspot.com.

they are just gobbledygook to your recipients. They may ignore your future emails. Instead, if you take some care with what you send out, not only do you build your experience by practice, but you can attract potential readers who may want to hear more from you, and so you develop your potential readership as your contacts grow.

6. Start with who knows you. If your church has a newsletter, offer to write a short piece or an announcement for an upcoming event. If your church doesn't have a newsletter, offer to start one. Since these are often done online, they will cost you nothing. But you gain an immediate readership. You can advertise your blog on it by simply putting it in your signature byline. This way, you do something positive for God's church while you also gather your readership.

7. Stay focused on your task—remember, it's all about building ideas with words. Once you've acquired some experience and a small reputation with your initial connections, then you can expand to reviews (like book or movie reviews), or articles, or stories, or poems, whichever is your talent. Books are often a series of linked articles. Stories are expanded to short stories, to novelettes, to novels.

For instance, the great Cape Cod storyteller Joseph C. Lincoln began by publishing short stories in popular magazines, then adapted some of the plots into novels and became a successful novelist. G. K. Chesterton's *Father Brown* mystery books are simply compilations of short stories he wrote for magazines. Edgar Rice Burroughs's iconic *Tarzan* books were magazine serials gathered into books. Few start big. It's like musicians say, "I was an overnight success—after ten years of performing in coffee shacks!"

8. Every opportunity to write is important. I say yes to almost all requests to contribute something, if I know anything about the topic and I can produce something in the deadline time. All requests, no matter how small, are in venues that are important to somebody, so they are important in themselves. No publication is too small, if we can contribute something that will please God by edifying an audience and, thereby, assisting God in reconciling the world (2 Cor 5:18–20). Then our effort is worthwhile, no matter how small the publication might be.

9. Don't dwell on yourself as your main topic: this is a warning to take seriously. That may seem strange to you, because you may have heard the saying, "There is a book in every person." Our own story is, indeed, the one

we know the best. We live with it every day, find it interesting, and want to tell it to everybody. So, it's what nearly every new author tries to do at first. But unless you're compiling your memoire for your grandchildren, or you just saved a famous movie star or some country's president from drowning, or you can explain without lying how you earned a trillion dollars last week while you were on vacation, or something of such great magnitude, you probably won't get published, especially if you haven't yet built your publishing resumé. Most of our life stories are as boring as watching snails race to everyone else. For example, as an experiment, try giving a detailed report to your friends of everything you did last month and count the yawns as you do so. Editors want to see that you can and will deliver something that is interesting to them and their readers and not just have their expectancy slaughtered with a piece that begins, "I was born as a child," and drones on.

So, how do we reconcile writing what we know best, our own stories, with what editors will accept? Make our stories about something that happened to us, or on a topic we're fairly sure we know about more thoroughly than others do and so will pull readers in.

In my estimation, here are some successful examples:

*The Corridors of Strange Darkness*

Eugene Neville was a pastor in Boston, so busy in ministry that he neglected having glaucoma treated. After he became blind, he wrote a book called *The Corridors of Strange Darkness: Struggling with the Experience of Glaucoma*. It is a heartrending report of his own experience with a warning to take care of the gift of sight that God has given us.

*Sharecropper to Entrepreneur to Pastor*

John Henry Womack told his tale in *Sharecropper to Entrepreneur to Pastor*, tracing how he rose from poverty as a child of field hands to become a business tycoon and, finally, a Boston pastor.

Worth noting is that both of these books were published by Wipf and Stock's Resource Publications imprint. Wipf and Stock has numerous book series; this particular line, however, is very hospitable to new authors and well worth new authors considering. According to the author guide,

> Since its inception, Resource Publications has been our imprint for both trade and academic works within a wide range of subject areas and target markets. Now listing over twenty-five hundred active titles, Resource Publications publishes within multiple genres including religion, psychology, fiction, poetry, memoir, biography, sermon collections, and more.[11]

11. Wipf and Stock Publishers, "Author Guide," 3.

My coeditor Jeanne DeFazio, whose interests are widely varied, has done several books with this imprint. Resource Publications is set up as what I like to call a "partnership publishing" co-op. The company and the author share the cost of production. For example, Wipf and Stock provides, at no cost to the author, the cover design and the author covers typesetting and printing. The author recovers the investment in book sales. On its side, W&S gives a generous discount on books to the author, and W&S pays royalties very responsibly and promotes the book for free.

Now, why would we want to release a book with which we would share the cost of production when the same publisher has other book lines where it assumes all expenses itself? Why pay anything when that's not required? The answer has to do with control. When a publisher pays everything, it, understandably, has the final word on title and content. It's taking the risks, so it can recommend strongly to change your proposed title. Sometimes, it exercises its right to insist. The author has input and can negotiate, and most publishers are open to that, but who pays the tab makes the decision. We supply a list of possible titles, but the publisher has put in its own title several times. Sometimes, we can get our own title in the subtitle, but the one who pays makes the rules.

We set up our House of Prisca and Aquila series with the blessing of John Wipf when there was a reluctance to publish evangelical egalitarian books across the industry. These kind of preference fads and trends pulse like waves on a sea. But with partnership publishing, we control content and are the responsible party for what we release, so we can have books published when we deem they are needed, despite the prevalent industry urgings. This does not mean, however, that W&S publishes anything in partnership publishing. It does not like proposals that viciously attack others. One author we knew proposed a book that had a negative view of a character who turned out to be based on a woman who had refused to marry him. The book was a tough city novel with enough good points to receive a chance. But when he sent in a sequel that was outright scurrilous to this character, W&S turned it down and rightly so. This is a mainstream publisher that will publish both sides of most debates, but, while an author can defend her or his side of that debate, character assassination, belittling of other views, and all the other dirty tricks of debate are not encouraged by this publisher.[12] It is a liberal Christian publisher that prefers positive

12. For an excellent reference on the dirty tricks of debate, see Seech, *Logic in Everyday Life.*

books and does not like scatological dismissals of those who disagree with their opponents.

Worth mentioning is that most of our books are published with Christian houses, most recently, Kregel as well as InterVarsity, Baker, SPCK (in England), and each time, we are so blessed with the graciousness of the staff. These are delightful people. But for such major publishers, the competition is very competitive. When we are choosing a publisher to approach with a project idea, we look for one that we think would be open to the topic of the book we're writing. The majority of our books, though not all, stem from our own interests.

My wife and I have established two book lines with Wipf and Stock: The House of Prisca and Aquila series, which focuses on Evangelical egalitarian topics designed to empower 100 percent of the church to use the leadership gifts the Holy Spirit has provided, and the Africanus Monograph Series for PhD dissertations. The second series is named for Julius Africanus, the great early church apologist, and both series are on the partnership model with the author receiving royalties (something not always granted to doctoral dissertations). We are also related to a third series, *Urban Voice*, founded by John Runyon, a dear friend and former GCTS colleague who now works at MIT, as does his equally brilliant wife, Eliana. All of these we brought to W&S. Our experiences with Wipf and Stock and its staff have been very positive and we have come to consider this company and its staff members as personal friends. Here are two books from one of our series that are pertinent to this section's topic, as each blends a personal story into a theme that will appeal to readers.

*Berkeley Street Theatre* and *The Christian World Liberation Front*

Our editor Jeanne DeFazio weaves in her own story as a California theater actress, with appearances on television and in film, in her two major books: the acclaimed *Berkeley Street Theatre: How Improvisation and Street Theater Emerged as a Christian Outreach to the Culture of the Time* and her best-seller *The Christian World Liberation Front: The Jesus Movement Model of Revival and Social Reform for the Postmodern Church.*

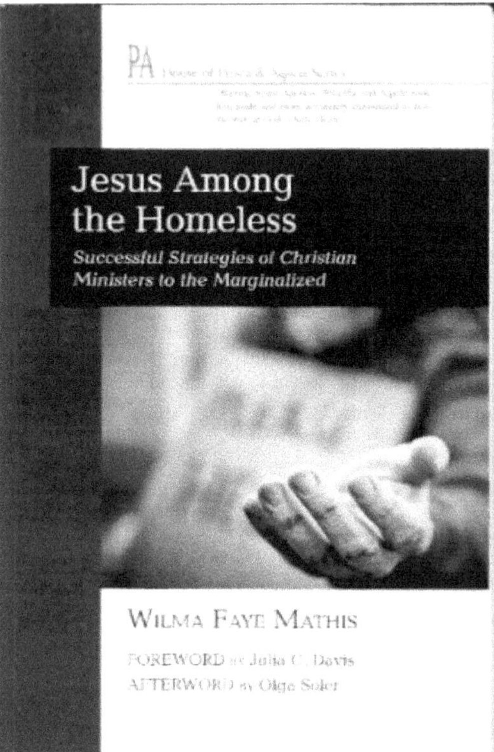


*Jesus Among the Homeless*

The Rev. Dr. Wilma Mathis also built her doctoral thesis into her ensuing book *Jesus Among the Homeless: Successful Strategies of Christian Ministers to the Marginalized*, out of her own experience in ministry to women in homeless shelters, a topic of great concern to all caring Christians.

In my case, I didn't mention myself much in my first several books until a publisher asked Aída and me to do a book on suffering. We weren't certain at first if we could tackle it. We prayed about it and felt led that we could do it, if we built it off the four biblical reasons she had discovered as she read through the Bible and was explaining in her class "Suffering and Joy in the New Testament." I used these four reasons to interpret the two devastating events that had derailed my birth family, the sudden accidental death of my sister and the work accident two years later that crippled my father. In this way, as I wrote up Aída's biblical insights and applied them to my own experience, addressing some of my own long-term unanswered questions, we were able to come up with our book *Joy Through the Night: Biblical Resources on Suffering.*

*Joy Through the Night*

This is the thirty-first year this book is in print, and it still, we are told, is helping people cope with life's reversals. Since this book was requested by the publisher and not envisioned by us, what we learned from that is we needed to look for a middle ground between what we want to write and what people want to read. Publishers often do know best.

True, we are all tempted to self-indulge, writing what we want to write, like maybe that experimental novel, which is so esoteric and complex, we think they'll just have to give us a prize; or that book on our favorite hobby, which has been neglected by everyone else and will open their eyes to just how much fun collecting old gas tank covers can really be; or our explanation of why all parents—and especially ours—should have let us drive as soon as we could see over the dashboard and began grabbing at the steering wheel . . . wait a minute! No one with any sense is going to write that one(!)—but you get the point. We can do a modicum of self-indulging, but we have to remember that writing, for us, is a ministry and should be pleasing God by advancing God's reign on earth, reaching people with what will help them advance in their faith and, thereby, pleasing acquisitions editors with a project that they can see will turn into a worthwhile and useful piece of work. This way, we won't waste our time and end up with a yellowing pile of dust-gathering paper, crinkling under an old flash drive for e-copies, tucked in the back of a box or drawer somewhere remote in our basement, attic, or—worst of all—lost in a storage unit on the edge of town.

10. In the previous section, I wrote a bit about choosing a publisher. Now, here's a warning: be very careful about publishing with what is called a "vanity press." This is a publishing house that charges you for everything. They might as well hold you up with a mask and a gun. They may soak you dry of thousands of dollars and you'll end up with nothing but a box of books in your basement. I heard a horrible account recently of a vanity press that charged a woman $1,000 and only gave her twenty books! They charged her $50 apiece! How could she ever sell those and recoup her costs?

Listen, if you are in a hurry and don't want to wait, with so many print-on-demand publishers available, similar to the options I mentioned in section 9, you don't need to be ripped off! Some print-on-demand publishers do pay for the book and are supposed to split the profit with you. But you have to work your way up to getting them interested. And be very careful to make sure the publisher keeps its end of the bargain.

An agent with whom I was working several years ago told me about a publisher with whom several of his other clients were working. The contracts were impressive. This publisher was offering a 65 percent royalty for established authors. Who offers that? Most of the time, new writers are sometimes offered 5 to 7.5 percent, and even regularly published authors receive 10 percent royalty and are glad to get it. So, this deal seemed too good to be true—a unique opportunity to cash in on one's own hard work. Or so it appeared. But it wasn't long before a lawsuit woke everyone to the fact that no royalties were ever paid, unless this publishing house initiated itself with a Ponzi scheme at the outset. When one client sued, he realized he had never received a signed copy of the publisher's contract. All of us signed our individual contracts and sent them in, but none of us ever received a signed contract back from the publisher. Despite what we were expecting, the reality was that this publisher would supply books for a discount and advertise our titles zealously, but sent us no royalties, keeping all the money from sales himself. Anything we earned we had to garner from our own sales. He might supply a certain amount of publicity, but no signed contract, so no payoff. The publisher had a thriving business. His authors were the most famous people in the poor house. So, make certain you get a contract that's signed before you deliver your whole manuscript.

Of course, print-on-demand publishers do exist who don't offer royalties, and that's okay if you already have a readership and only expect to earn your keep from your own sales. But this arrangement should be made very clear to you at the outset. If you can sell your books successfully yourself, you can save the money you might have spent having them printed.

And don't forget university presses. They are getting into the competitive side on all types of writing. When the publisher of *Mysterium and Mystery* (my first book, which was adapted from my doctoral dissertation) terminated its academic line, the editors wanted to keep my book in print because it was selling and had been called definitive in its field. The company refused and I received two offers, one from a well-known trade publisher who would put me in the big time and Southern Illinois University Press.

*Mysterium and Mystery*

Southern Illinois offered me $1,000 to go with it. I asked the big company editor what she would do if she were me. She said, "Take the money, because they'll keep your book in print to earn the advance back." University presses are right in the center of the action these days. They have the money and the prestige. And the editors at both Southern Illinois and Temple's University presses were delightful to work with.

11. Build your own readership: in this day of social networking and excessive competition, you really do have to attract your own clientele. For shy writers, this is often very difficult. Some well-known publishers are now demanding a list of at least two thousand people willing to buy your book before they'll take it. So, I repeat, today's writers have to build their own following. You are the best sales representative for your own work. It used to be easy to speak at churches or senior centers or libraries if you had something interesting to say, but COVID killed that for a long time. We ourselves just had our first and second invitation to speak after a long layoff where we sold a few books after our presentations, so opportunities may be slowly beginning once again. Of course, there are always YouTube shows. Jeanne is proficient at these. I think your e-books would sell best to net-oriented readers, and especially to readers in other countries.

12. Write about what you know. I know about inner city ministry and theology and New Jersey, Kentucky, Puerto Rico, and the Dominican Republic—the places I've lived. I also know about Jamaica because my wife and I taught there on and off for a decade, so I've met the Rastafari and I take their opinions and their music and lyrics very seriously. Out of the many interviews I recorded in reasoning with them came my book on their variety of views of the Lord, *Dread Jesus*, which was published by SPCK, England's oldest religious publishing house.

*Dread Jesus*

After twelve years, Wipf and Stock bought the rights, and, today, it is in print with Wipf and Stock here in the USA, as are so many of our other titles. Before I finished *Dread Jesus*, I also did a side project with two Caribbean scholars. I named it *Chanting Down Babylon: The Rastafari Reader*. This 467-page work became a best-selling book and is universally considered the definitive multi-author work on Rastafari, thanks to a book review declaring it so in *Kingston's Sunday Gleaner*, Jamaica's premier newspaper. It's also the only book of mine that I've seen being sold in an airport!

*Chanting Down Babylon*

These books taught me that to work on two related books and finish one while the other is still in process is possible. One book can lead to another. Writing is not necessarily a linear process. And, yes, you can pause to write an article, or some blog posts, or a presentation, or a sermon, as happened with these two. But, at the same time, there is an inspiration that I feel comes on me as I am working on a piece and it's easy to have it vanish when I get sidetracked. Once that motivating drive is gone, it's hard to get it back.

Also, for professionals in any field that demands you write to move forward, you do well to center your efforts on projects related to your job to keep a paycheck coming in. My field is theology and the arts. So, while I'm doing these kinds of projects, I'm also writing in my field on topics mostly about theology interacting with the arts. So, my book *Three in One: Analogies for the Trinity* is an analysis of the illustrations we use when we try to describe the Trinity in teaching our Sunday school classes or witnessing to someone considering the faith. With this book as our guide, we can discern what's good in our imagery and we can skip what's bad.

*Three in One: Analogies for the Trinity*

So, what I'm trying to show you is a connection here: as exotic as *Dread Jesus* and *Chanting Down Babylon* may appear, they and *Three in*

*One* are intrinsically related. How so? They are each about theology and the arts—in one case, music; the other, imagery—because that's what I know and enjoy. Further, since my title at Gordon-Conwell Theological Seminary is distinguished adjunct professor of theology and the arts, that's the area I am expected to engage in my writing.

So, my advice to you is, before you tackle a project, ask yourself, what do I know best? How is my life involved in this interest, and what do I want to share from it? At the same time, what do I not know about that I should leave to others?

Now, here's what I don't know about: outer space, the old West, Amish romances, deep sea diving, and a lot of other stuff. I leave those alone for other writers who know about them.[13]

13. Therefore, along with target topics to write about, each of us should also target an audience of people who share our interests as potential readers for our work. For myself, I write my nonfiction books to use in class for my seminary students. They are my primary audience. I have taught over 3,600 of them. I also have in mind informed lay readers, so I try to define all the technical terms I use. I tend to write my articles in systematic theology for my academic colleagues, and I submit them to academic journals. These days, I mainly put them into *Africanus Journal* to support the journal we created for Gordon-Conwell. I write my fiction for my friends. I keep in mind stories I would enjoy reading myself and ones I think friends and acquaintances would enjoy, too. I put poems in the front of each of my books, and, over the years, I've had the privilege of having them published in journals like *Christianity and Literature* and *Priscilla Papers*, and we even put one on our blog. Hunting for the right place to submit and finding that pot of gold will be well worth the search. Years ago, *Christianity Today*, which had printed several of my articles, published my poem "Angel of Death Lay Down Your Sword" and a talented and enterprising musician made it the basis of an oratorio. You just never know what will happen to your work once you let it go.

One very helpful reminder of having a target audience is Luke writing his gospel to Theophilus, as my former agent Les Stobbe explained in his insightful article, "Earning the Right to be Published," which you can

13. I may not write in these areas, but I do read in them, e.g. my newest favorite sci-fi stories these days are Bruce I McDaniel's *Child of Covar Child of Earth* (2021) and its sequel *Alien Son* (2025).

read free online in the 2018 November issue of *Africanus Journal* (10:2, pp. 4–11).

*Africanus Journal*

Les, who was an editor as well as a writer and agent, has also written a very interesting book about his successful writing career, which he titled *God Moments in My Publishing Life: The Making of a Writer and Publisher*, which is well worth reading.[14]

14. Make rereading, revising, and rewriting an essential part of your writing discipline. I reread my manuscripts over and over and over again. Then I revise, revise, and revise. In fiction, for example, I try to get all the days my characters are living in my story coordinated, just as days flow along in our daily lives.

15. So, outlines are essential for creating both fiction and nonfiction. My wife and I use annotated outlines, gathering up copious notes. In fiction, she does cast biographies and designs cities and places the characters

14. Stobbe, *Making of a Writer and Publisher*; this book is available from EABooks Publishing, a division of Living Parables of Central Florida.

will inhabit, and for both fiction and nonfiction, I gather up a huge amount of relevant data all grouped in successive file folders, one for each chapter we project in our outline. By the time writing comes, I write up these annotated outlines and invent new characters, and new plot twists, and any other additions in the spirit of the outline she has put together.

So, our manuscripts go through many revisions. I spent four mornings crafting one important paragraph in our jointly written novel *Cave of Little Faces*.

I wrote that pivotal paragraph and rewrote it, shifting it around and back again in one way and then another way, and then around again. Then I left it and came back the next day and reorganized it, and then did it again the next until it was right. Why? Because that's what a writer does: writes to get it right.

16. Once you do get it right, let it go. What GK Chesterton said of a dog and a law is true with a book or any writing project as well: "If you let loose a law, it will do as a dog does; it will obey its own nature, not yours. Such sense as you have put into the law (or the dog) will be fulfilled. But you will not be able to fulfill a fragment of anything you have forgotten to put in it."[15]

17. Manage your time well. Figure out how much time you have to finish well, but, at the same time, unless you're writing *Gone with the Wind*, don't spend a lifetime on it. I have a friend who was writing a book when I met him some thirty years ago, and he's still working on it. There's no end in sight. Get it done! Your heirs may opt for the dumpster.

18. But, at the same time, we shouldn't be in such a hurry that we overwork and stress out and let our project become onerous to us. When we can't stand it anymore, and we're just writing to get it done, readers can tell. When we get bored, they get bored. And, when they get bored, they are soon gone.

Instead, pay attention to what we could call the "seven shoulds." We should take a break and relax. Writing should be enjoyable for us. In fact, it should be fun. We should be looking forward to it. We should think of our manuscript as a garden of words we want to see flourish. We should take the time to think of delightful ways of putting our thoughts into words. We should keep shaping sentences up until we can smile and say, "Oh, I like that!"

15. Chesterton, "Lawlessness of Lawyers," 172.

To accomplish this positive regimen, we need time for sustained thought. If we can avoid rushing to bang stuff out just to beat a deadline to get something in hand or in print, we will have time to polish our work and make it something in which we can delight. Even a good grocery list takes time! I've heard some writers say, "I hate writing, but I like having written." If you hate writing so much, why do it? Find another job you'll actually enjoy!

Essential, then, to lower the stress and maximize the delight, is to work ahead of deadlines. Don't leave them to the last minute. This is your life; don't live it in self-inflicted misery.

I've mentioned *Cave of Little Faces* a couple of times now because I love this novel. When we wrote it, we had so much fun. We were staying one January in the Dominican Republic, where my wife was born. So, we visited all the localities we mentioned in the manuscript, and sometimes invented new names for them and even created our own city in the midst of them for our center of action. This way, some of our own actual adventures, like the highway we were driving suddenly disappearing in front of us into a lake and our car, in neutral, mysteriously being drawn backwards up a hill by a magnetic force in the terrain, could become our characters' experiences, too.

So, we put together a working outline of the plot. Then, each morning, I woke up early and wrote up a chapter following the plot outline, sometimes expanding a single sentence into an entire chapter, adding new events and characters as I needed them to fill out the plot, and that's how our succinct thirteen-proposed-chapter outline turned into a fifty-chapter rip-roaring adventure.

Each morning, I read Aída the chapter I had just written and she critiqued it, suggesting improvements. We'd negotiate, of course, but I benefitted from all her insights, and we'd revise the chapter together. Then, each afternoon, she customized the manuscript following the changes we had penciled in that morning. One afternoon, she even wrote in a new chapter to expand what we needed. The whole process was very enjoyable and readers have told us that a feeling of exhilaration is present throughout the book. One told us that, when she finished the book, the sudden realization that these characters would no longer be with her with new adventures made her sad. They had become that real to her.

With our co-written nonfiction, we write separately, dividing up different parts of a book, and then edit each other's contribution. We also edit each other's separate books. I believe that a communal spirit like this when writing also reaches out to our readers and helps include them as a valued part of the entire experience of the book, just like any communal effort has the potential to involve others.

19. Make your book something you want to read yourself. Remember this rule: if you're not enjoying yourself while you're writing, your reader may find what you wrote stultifying.

20. Ultimately, your work is about excellence, and no short cut to excellence exists.

21. Always remember when writing your manuscript that, within your target audience, your acquisitions editors are among your most important readers. When you write your précis, which is the letter that will accompany your sample chapter and tell the main point(s) of your piece and what you hope it will achieve, you should include your answers to the questions an acquisitions editor is expecting you to answer, so let's consider these.

## The Seven Questions Acquisition Editors Have Asked Us

1. Why is this book necessary? Times are hard for publishers. The competition for our attention seems overwhelming. So, they are looking for the diamond in the mine. Give them a convincing defense why your book will shine on their shelves and be of great attraction to readers and great value to everyone.

2. What makes the book you are proposing different enough to be considered? Don't hesitate to tell the editor why you think the book you are writing is different from all other books on the same topic. If you give a well-thought-through answer, you will also demonstrate your proficiency in your field. Feature in your presentation why what you are exploring and writing is unique to your book and stands out or supplements what is missing in other writers' books. Do this graciously as you reference other books. Your point is to make your work stand out and demonstrate why you are uniquely qualified to write this idea up.

3. Who is your target audience? I told you earlier how I visualize my audience. How do you visualize yours?

4. Have you added in at least one sample chapter, up to three (depending on the length of each)? These show the editor what your writing is like. Also, make sure you send along an outline of your content. Doing this will map out your work in the minds of the editorial team. It tells the prospective publisher how you are planning to put your article or story or book together. It foreshadows what you will flesh out. For nonfiction writing, this is imperative, especially for books. All acquisitions editors want to see a working table of contents and often an annotated outline: a short summary of what you will be researching and writing and a sentence or two of how that chapter will move forward the argument that is central to your book. The information you offer should include the tentative length you project for your entire proposed piece and the deadline you suggest for the completion and delivery of your work. The next two points will deal with these two essential issues.

5. On the question of what is your estimate of your coming submission's page count, keep in mind that length can be a deal-breaker! For books and articles, in these cyber-dominated days, more and more publishers will want to handle mostly articles of about 15 to 20 pages and books of about 140 pages when they are printed. Fewer and fewer publishers will accept a manuscript over 100,000 words. Maximum book length should be 277 pages, but you fare better if you can make yours less than that, for example, 250 pages. All I can add is I'm glad I wrote my longer books when I did. While some do still release giant tomes, for most of us, "Write short" is the advice in today's fortune cookie.

6. Will you stay on deadline? Editors want to know, what is your actual time estimate for delivering your production? If you get a contract, it will have a deadline with which you have agreed. Adhering to your contract stipulations is imperative. Publishers take these deadlines very seriously. If you don't make your deadline, it fouls up their production schedule. Your book is an investment for their company. If you don't deliver by the deadline, that raises havoc with their projected printing plans. The publisher might relegate your piece to the end of its current time scheme for publishing and may postpone printing your article or launching your book into the shadowy mist of months away.

7. How will you market your book? Authors marketing their books is now a key element in all negotiations. Competition is ferocious these days with

so many books being hawked on the net that marketing is an essential part of whether publishers will risk putting your book in print. They want to know whom you will ask to endorse it, whom you will ask to promote it; in fact, they routinely ask for a list of names and addresses and will send these people you listed free copies of your book, expecting them, on your word, to write reviews on it, require your book in their classes, recommend it on Goodreads. In short, you need to be gathering up this support base ahead of time, so you will show your publisher you are going to do your part to move your book into readers' hands. This is where blog posts come in handy. In summary, a key goal of the marketing wing is to have endorsers who will actually agree to promote your book and unlock a market for it. Essentially, you are committing your list of people in the field in which you are hoping to sell your book to be promoters, who will give you positive reviews that will make readers want to check your book out, or put you on their radio shows and interview you, or recommend your book to their colleagues, and so on. Make sure you have really contacted each of them and they are loyal and on your side.

One serious warning: be careful not to ask someone famous you don't know to review your book. He or she may end up annoyed and give you a scathing review. From time to time, this happens at our journal. Writers pursue a well-known person in the field who ends up trashing their books. We try to have each hostile reviewer tone it down a bit but are not always successful. One really terrible review can kill your book. You end up worse off then if you had just looked for somebody not famous whom you know, for example, a colleague who likes you and your work. Nothing is magical about this. It's akin to looking for a job and having a potential employer asking you for a reference from someone with whom you've worked already. You don't pick that obnoxious boss who fired you, when you were late for work, because you were blocked by an accident in the tunnel, and you had no reception available to explain traffic was backed up—right? This is why we all have friends: we look out for them; they look out for us.

## So, Now That You Have a Game Plan, How Do You Meet Acquisitions Editors?

The answers to this enigma are as varied as the twists and turns in life itself: a combination of planned and providential encounters.

In my own experience, my invitation to have my first book published came about in a very circuitous way. My wife and I had been invited to train seminarians in city ministry and teach some courses for an evangelical track set up for New York Theological Seminary by a friend, Rev. Bill Iverson. The way that came about was that I had worked four years earlier, in the summer of 1970, with Bill's Cross Counter ministry, helping city churches relate to their neighborhoods after the riot in Newark, New Jersey, had left Springfield Avenue looking like a war zone. As God's providence organized that summer, Aída, who was then my fiancée, was also in Newark independently working with Model Cities to address the same needy area.

Two years later, Bill performed our wedding ceremony, and two years after that, in 1974, we were back in Newark, teaching in his program for training seminarians. Aída and I were both finishing master of theology (ThM) degrees, just one step over the students we were teaching.

As new professors, we joined the Evangelical Theological Society and went to its conferences. At one of these, I proposed a book project to an editor, who gave me a very firm reality check. He said, "Our books are written by PhDs. Why would we publish a book by someone without a doctorate?" Hmm, that made sense. I had no answer to that. So, when our family was finally settled at Gordon-Conwell Theological Seminary in 1983, I started on a doctor of theology degree, which is technically the next degree above a PhD. It requires the usual comprehensive and language exams but an unusual twelve, rather than eight, courses demanded, since it is inter-field, so a candidate must gain an expertise in two fields (mine were theology and ancient literature, working in the Greek apocrypha on which I was examined). Further, the school I chose, Boston University School of Theology (BUSTh), at that time had an unusual policy. The normal PhD dissertation is expected to be around 300 pages. BUSTh was noted for long dissertations. Mine was 826 pages. And it provided the way; my goal to get a doctorate to get a book in print was reached.

University Microfilms had momentarily set up its own academic line of carefully selected dissertations and asked me if it could publish mine. It turned out to be their sixth and last book in this experiment. I had written on the question of how the great mystery of God had become the secular mystery novel. When the book was published, it caused a sensation. It had numerous reviews (including a very gracious one by J. I. Packer) and that was how my writing ministry with books began. At the height of *Mysterium and Mystery*'s success, University Microfilms canceled its academic experiment and everything went out of print. The editors pleaded for my book to remain by itself because it was selling, but the line was over. My book was the last to go, and then its print-run sold out and the book languished as unavailable for three years until Southern Illinois University Press put it back in print. While the parade had now marched on, it has still managed to wave its little flag.

While I took projects around to the booths at conferences and showed them to publishers, many of my other earliest books came only by invitation. Zondervan needed a commentary on 2 Corinthians to finish a series when the author working on it was suddenly sidelined by a health issue. The publisher called around to the seminaries and a colleague recommended my wife, who was teaching a course on that book of the Bible and doing a first-rate job. Being a brand-new professor at Gordon-Conwell Theological Seminary, she was still creating her courses as she was teaching them, so her time was limited. I had less of a teaching load for health issues, so I wrote up her class notes and added in my own exegetical insights here and there, and we made the deadline. She now had her own textbook to use in class and I had two books come out in 1989, my shortened dissertation and this commentary in English and in Chinese as well. What I learned is that books can germinate out of circumstances in life.

Once publishers get to know you and see that you will deliver, the opportunities begin to come. We did the *Prayer Life of Jesus* next, based on a course on prayer I was asked to teach for Gordon-Conwell. So, we based it on my notes for this course. That book is still in print since 1990.

When a professor at Gordon College, who was doing a book on suffering for InterVarsity Press, had to give up the project, another colleague graciously suggested we could do it. My wife was teaching a course on suffering and joy in the New Testament, so we pooled our ideas, and I wrote a draft based on the four reasons for suffering she had discovered in the Bible and applied these findings by contextualizing them as interpretive tools to apply to my own family's catastrophes of my sister's accidental death and my father's crippling work accident. These were unresolved traumatic disasters from my youth, the first when I was six and the second two years later when I turned eight, and they had blighted our lives since then. Our family was also plagued by miscarriages and stillborns, and so my parents' projected hope for children was reduced to just me, a sickly little boy as the only survivor. This book helped me sort all that out and is still in print now with Wipf and Stock, helping others. The advice we always hear is we should write about what we know. What we live is what we know. As we discovered earlier, our infirmities and setbacks and disadvantages may be the stuff with which we can build a better life, as we reach for wholeness and take our readers with us.

The next providential moment came in a line at a restaurant. Aída and I were presenting papers at an *Evangelical Theological Society* conference in Florida, being housed in a hotel that looked to us Yankees like it was situated in the everglades. No other buildings were around it. This hotel was surrounded by mud and its hostess must have been hired from the local penitentiary. She was terrifying. "How many???" she'd snap. "Two," would quaver some shocked scholar and spouse. "Stand over there," she'd dismiss them and then shout, "Next!" On an inspiration, I turned to the lone man behind us and asked, "Do you want to eat with us?" "You'll let me eat with you?" he gasped, the light of life coming back into his eyes. "You bet!" "How many???" snapped the fury. "Three," I said. She paused for a split second, eyeing us closely. I grinned, trying to look charming. "Take that table over there!" she barked curtly. And we were dismissed from her presence, slipping quickly around the small table she'd indicated with a toss of her head. Our seatmate turned out to be John Wipf. We had read about him and his enterprising action to start publishing new books in his bookstore warehouse. Aída asked him if he'd be interested in an idea we had to publish PhD dissertations for students we were coaching through their PhD studies at other schools, since GCTS at that point had no PhD program as it is now initiating. I asked him if he would consider a book line we were thinking about tentatively to be called "The House of Prisca and Aquila," a series of egalitarian books seeking to empower 100 percent of the Christian church, orthodox, evangelical women, as well as men, to use the gifts the Holy Spirit had given them. We all paused. I asked, "Would you be interested in either?" "I'll take them both!" he said. Even today, as I think about that seminal encounter, that great New Jersey patois salute jumps forward in my mind when I meet or even think about John Wipf: "I luv dis guy!" At least, that's how it's said in the movies. Today, we are still publishing with Wipf and Stock, working not only with those two series but with a third one, John Runyan's "Urban Voice." Together, these series have put out nearly forty books for a variety of authors.

Another serendipitous experience happened to a friend when he was chatting with a neighbor. He mentioned a manuscript he was working on, only to discover his new acquaintance was an acquisitions editor with a well-known publisher—can you imagine that? So, he told him all about the book he had been writing and the editor got enthused about it.

For fiction writers, the place to turn can be as intentional as attending an event of the American Christian Fiction Writers (ACFW) organization. This active group has conferences, contests, and regional support groups for members. I've belonged to it for years, although I am so busy writing nonfiction, I have only gotten around to submitting one novel to their contest, and I didn't win anything. But one of these days, I really want to go to one of their conferences. Les Stobbe, who, as I mentioned, had been my agent before he retired, urged me to go. I still want to take that good advice when I can find the time.

Some have opted for the University of Iowa's "Iowa Writers' Workshop," which is legendary and opens doors for the truly gifted. I only know about it by reputation, but U of I specializes in creative writing programs and is very famous, if one has the time and money. If one can't go anywhere, writing programs of excellence may be all around and feature visits by editors you can meet.

What I am saying here is pray and work hard. Attend conferences along the lines of your interests. Go to the booths. Talk to the representatives there. Let them get to know you and submit ideas to them, even if they don't take them. Keep writing and publishing in venues that are available. God's providential moments happen in these contexts. But you have to be there so the Holy Spirit will open the opportunity for you. As we used to encourage each other during the Jesus Movement, "God won't drive a parked car."

## Conclusion

In this chapter, I shared advice on how to prepare to write. I gave you writing hints for gaining a hearing, my wife and I provided a questionnaire for editing your work, and I gave suggestions on how to proceed, if your goal is being published. I also coached you on what to submit to an acquisitions editor and included the kind of questions acquisitions editors have asked my wife and me. I also added in the key elements of what to put in the précis letter, which should accompany your sample chapter and include a summary of your submission's main points. I illustrated all these points with my personal experience of how things worked out for me, putting in everything I could think to put in so your quest might work out for you, too.

Now, here is the main point I hope every reader will take away from this chapter. If we feel led to please God by edifying people through our writing, we can write as a means to expand our ministry. But, since there is no short cut to excellence, all of us need to write with care, so that we can present our best work to the Lord and, in that way, do our part to advance God's reign in this world. May God bless you thoroughly and help you flourish in this high calling.

Find Dr. Spencer's lecture from the seminar in the bibliography: DeFazio, "The Digital Evangelist: Expanding Your Ministry by Writing for Publication."

PART TWO

# Digitally Evangelizing by Building Your Autobiographical Testimony Around a Theme

Jeanne C. DeFazio

# Chapter Two

# Expanding Your Ministry by Publishing Your Testimony

Jeanne DeFazio

THANKS TO DR. SPENCER for including my book *The Christian World Liberation Front* (CWLF) as recommended reading. I had the honor to be an Athanasian Scholar in his Systematic Theology Courses for fifteen years. Without his advice and encouragement, I would not be an author. In the thirteen years since my first publication, I have improved my writing skills, been privileged to publish through the Spencers' House of Prisca and Aquila series of Wipf and Stock Publishing, and have learned a lot by navigating the submission process.

CWLF represents the history genre featured in this present book. The subtitle of that book is *The Jesus Movement's Model of Revival and Reform For The Postmodern Church*. CWLF was featured in *Time Magazine*'s June 21, 1971, iconic psychedelic Jesus edition:

> Nothing except Christ makes waves at gatherings of Berkeley's Christian World Liberation Front, which was in the vanguard of the movement in the San Francisco Bay Area. CWLF Bible meetings are like an understanding embrace: the members sit naturally in a rough circle; a spaced-out speed freak crawls in, is casually accepted, and kneels; a baby plays; the only black plucks a guitar, and the group swings easily into a dozen songs. The hat is passed with a new invitation: 'If you have something to spare, give; if you need, take.' Finally they rise, take one another's hands, and sing 'We will walk with each other / We will walk hand in hand / And they'll know we are Christians by our love.'[1]

1. DeFazio, *Christian World Liberation Front*, 13; DeFazio, "Alternative Jesus," 5.

You have to write about what you know. Some CWLF members came to Jesus out of drug addictions and cults. CWLF member Brooks Alexander personalized his testimony beautifully:

> The whole ambiguous and unsatisfactory story of my life came to a singular head one night in October, as I sat, stoned and alone, staring into a fireplace full of ashes. I saw inescapably what my situation really was. I understood that despite all the true things I had discovered, I had never come close to the truth. I knew that despite all the movement in my life, not only had I failed to arrive, I wasn't even really on the path. More frightening than anything else, I saw that I had gradually discarded the objects of my caring, one by one. I had begun with a concern for many things and large issues; I was left with the vestiges of a very small and self-centered itch of hedonistic ambition, and even that was perceptibly slipping away. I understood instinctively that when that was gone, I would have no real reason to go on living even for a single day. Clearly, something had to change. Just as clear was the fact that the change had to be qualitative, and not merely quantitative (i.e., more-of-the-same-but-better was not good enough). As far as I understood what was happening that night (due mostly to the concepts I had absorbed from the Eastern religions), I thought that I was reaching down deep inside myself in an attempt to tap some positive source of energy that I visualized to be in there. What actually happened seems (in retrospect) to be that God interpreted the whole situation as a prayer for help.[2]

You can see why the book rang true for the readers who experienced the 1960s and '70s. Being a member of CWLF's Berkeley Street Theatre transformed my life. When you write about something you experienced that made a difference in your life, you have a better shot at impacting readers.

Dr. William Spencer guided me to write the CWLF book by collecting testimonies from my lifelong CWLF friends and recommended that I include Stephen Sparks' iconic photographs.

2. DeFazio, *Christian World Liberation Front*, 21.

CWLF members at a People's Park demonstration.

Dr. Spencer contributed an afterword to the CWLF book that contained unique primary sources. As the book's back cover summary explains,

> This book is a retrospective and model for the postmodern church for revival and reform containing actual primary source quotations from all those involved. It is a unique primary source history of Jesus Movement reflections and not just another secondary book. There is nothing like it available on this seminal, significant, and influential ministry.[3]

The book is a "tweener"; it's in between an academic work and a general read. Submitting the manuscript and revising it with the publisher's copy editors was a lot of work, requiring discipline and focus on grammar, clarity, and organization of ideas. This endless detail work is the sacrificial part of publishing. Thanks to Dr. Spencer's mentoring, the CWLF book is my most popular book. The testimonies and photos resonate with baby boomers.

I want to encourage students and colleagues to publish their personal experiences that drew them to Jesus, and to quote Scripture because Isa 55:11 promises, "So is my word that goes out from my mouth: It will not return to me empty, but will accomplish what I desire and achieve the purpose for which I sent it."

In conclusion, CWLF reaped a harvest of flower children who looked for love in all the wrong places until they found Jesus, the Lover of their souls. CWLF leader Jack Sparks, a former college professor, baptized

3. DeFazio, *Christian World Liberation Front*, back cover.

hippies in Sproul Plaza's Ludwig's Fountain. As Julia Davis explains in CWLF's foreword,

> The Christian World Liberation Front modeled scripturally based revival and reform. CWLF members regarded Scripture as 'historically accurate, and consistent in itself, fully reliable, and authoritative as God's revelation.' (HPA Mission Statement). Jack Sparks held a PhD from the University of Iowa and taught research and design in the educational psychology department at Penn State University and debated with Berkeley intellectuals as an equal; he was also a holy man who esteemed and revered Scripture as the word of God.[4]

Why was CWLF so successful? Jack Sparks preached the word of God, as the apostle Paul counseled his young mentee Timothy in his letter,

> Preach the word; be prepared in season and out of season; correct, rebuke and encourage—with great patience and careful instruction. For the time will come when people will not put up with sound doctrine. Instead, to suit their own desires, they will gather around them a great number of teachers to say what their itching ears want to hear. They will turn their ears away from the truth and turn aside to myths. But you, keep your head in all situations, endure hardship, do the work of an evangelist, discharge all the duties of your ministry." (1 Tim 4:2–5)

CWLF members boldly shared their testimonies: "They triumphed over him by the blood of the Lamb and by the word of their testimony; they did not love their lives so much as to shrink from death" (Rev 12:11).

Today, we should take to heart Shane Pruitt's wise advice: "More than 57% of the total global population is on social media. That's a massive digital mission field with potential for Great Commission harvest!"[5]

We should post all our stories on social media and let people know why we opened our hearts to receive Jesus as Lord and Savior and how his forgiveness and unconditional love changed our lives. I thank all of these Christian authors who allowed their stories to be published to encourage others. God bless you as you join us and publish to bring the lost to Jesus before his return.

4. DeFazio, *Christian World Liberation Front*, xiv.

5. Pruitt, "Five Ways to Use," para. 1.

Jeanne DeFazio is a former SAG/AFTRA (Screen Actors Guild/American Federation of Television and Radio Artists) actress of Spanish-Italian descent, who played supporting parts in theater, movies, and television series, then served the marginalized in the drama of real life. She became a teacher of second language-learner children in the barrios of San Diego. She completed a BA in history at the University of California, Davis, MA in theology at Gordon-Conwell Theological Seminary, and a Cal State Teach English Language Learners program. From 2009 to 2024, she served as an Athanasian teaching scholar at Gordon-Conwell's multicultural Boston Center for Urban Ministerial Education.

Julia C. Davis attending the 2018 Athanasian scholars dinner.

## Chapter Three

# How I Expanded My Ministry by Publishing

Julia C. Davis

I am honored to participate in *The Digital Evangelist: Expanding Your Ministry by Writing for Publication*. I am an African American educator and pastor. Since March 2020, when COVID-19 was officially declared a pandemic, I have expanded my ministry as a contributing author to ten books. These books are available on Amazon, featured in Google Books, and for sale on Walmart online. I spoke in panel discussions via Zoom (along with my fellow contributing authors) that were uploaded to YouTube and viewed internationally. The *Africanus Journal* published reviews of these books. I was privileged to contribute a forward to *Jesus Among the Homeless* and *The Christian World Liberation Front*. Both of these two books were recommended reading for "The Digital Evangelist" seminar. As I reflect on what I wrote in both books, I realize that George Floyd's death and the riots and violence that followed motivated me to speak up. I wanted to do more than put a sign at my front door that said, "Black Lives Matter."

I participate gladly in House of Prisca and Aquila projects because HPA's mission statement resonates with my core Christian beliefs. I stand on the Bible as "God's revelation that affects both thoughts and words, so it is plenary, historically accurate, and consistent in itself, fully reliable, and authoritative as God's revelation" (House of Prisca and Aquila Mission Statement).[1]

What I love most about Wilma Mathis's *Jesus Among the Homeless* is that it identifies strategies to help the marginalized based on scriptural principles. For example, in "Empowering the Practical Lives of Homeless Women Through Transformational Journaling," Dr. Mathis states, "We are

1. House of Prisca and Aquila, "About Us," para. 1.

instructed to care for widows and orphans (including the homeless)."[2] James 1:27 declares, "Religion that God our Father accepts as pure and spotless is this, to look after orphans and widows in their distress and to keep oneself from being polluted by the world."[3] Dr. Mathis identifies biblical journaling as a strategy to help homeless women: "Since journaling plays a positive role in aiding recovery from drug addiction, biblical transformational journaling can also play positive roles in helping homeless women."[4] Joshua 1:8 explains, "This Book of the Law shall not depart from your mouth, but you shall meditate on it day and night, so that you may be careful to do according to all that is written in it. For then you will make your way prosperous, and then you will have good success."[5]

As a contributing author to *Empowering English Language Learners*, I explained why and how I taught Christian principles, particularly forgiveness without retribution, in a politically correct fashion for the inner-city public school system:

> In over thirty years teaching racially diverse inner-city students, I applied scriptural and constitutional principles developing strategies that empowered students to mobilize and succeed in predominantly white institutions of higher education. So many of these students have acquired professional status and make a difference in their own lives and within their communities.[6]

Scripturally based "classroom rules" are a way to bring the knowledge of Christian principles into the public-school classroom without being "politically incorrect." My students begin each class by devising classroom principles. When students have written the classroom rules, they are more apt to abide by them.

For example, "I am ready to be respectful and responsible and a good classroom citizen" reflects the values of Ps 19:14, Prov 18:24, and Mark 12:31. "Listening without interrupting" describes the wisdom of Prov 18:2. "Speaking without accusing" is a mandate of Jas 1:19. "Answering with-out arguing" is an instruction of Prov 17:1. Ephesians 4:15 outlines the importance of "sharing." "Forgiveness without retribution" is a mandate of Col 3:13.[7]

2. Mathis, *Jesus Among the Homeless*, 78.
3. Mathis, *Jesus Among the Homeless*, xiii.
4. Mathis, *Jesus Among the Homeless*, 79.
5. Mathis, *Jesus Among the Homeless*, xiv.
6. DeFazio, *Commission*, xi–xii.
7. DeFazio and Spencer, *Empowering English Language Learners*, 40–41. All Scripture

I modeled educational strategies (based on scriptural principles) to promote inclusion and identified how to stand on the word of God to overcome prejudice and promote peaceful coexistence.

When you publish, I also recommend that you write about what you know and back up every statement with scriptural principles and include a reference to God's word. Isaiah 55:11 promises, "So is my word that goes out from my mouth: It will not return to me empty, but will accomplish what I desire and achieve the purpose for which I sent it."

Jeanne DeFazio models building Christian community for the homeless, describing a monthly meeting at a McDonald's restaurant she organized in New York City from 1989 to 1995.[8] Jeanne's chapter identifies two key strategies based on scriptural principles: feeding the homeless ("Do not forget to show hospitality to strangers, for by doing so some people have shown hospitality to angels without knowing it" [Heb 13:2][9]) and providing pastoral support and spiritual encouragement for them ("For everything that was written in the past was written to teach us, so that through the endurance taught in the Scriptures and the encouragement they provide we might have hope" [Rom 15:4][10]).

Martha Reyes, in "The Hosanna Foundation," explains how her counseling guidelines for the depressed and anxious are rooted in the promises of Jesus' words: "Peace I leave with you; my peace I give you. I do not give to you as the world gives. Do not let your hearts be troubled and do not be afraid" (John 14:27).[11] In her afterword, "Those Without a Home," Olga Soler identifies Scriptures mandating believers to mentor the homeless: "Where there is no guidance, a people falls, but in an abundance of counselors there is safety" (Prov 11:14 ESV).[12]

As for my own experience ministering to the homeless, I wrote,

> I relate to these experienced ministers to the marginalized. I volunteer in downtown Boston praying with the homeless, distributing food and Bibles to them. As a chaplain, I have clearance to minister in hospitals and prisons. Jesus is at work through me as I pray at the bedside of a battered homeless woman and with

verses referenced in this quote are from the NIV translation of the Bible.

8. DeFazio and Lathrop, *Creative Ways*, 7–9.
9. Mathis, *Jesus Among the Homeless*, 60.
10. Mathis, *Jesus Among the Homeless*, xiv.
11. Mathis, *Jesus Among the Homeless*, xiv.
12. Mathis, *Jesus Among the Homeless*, xiv.

> inmates. I recommend that everyone read this book and take the scriptural principles in it to heart. Strategies based on God's word heal and transform lives.[13]

Another opportunity to share my story came in a book I did with Jeanne DeFazio and Wilma Mathis, *An Artistic Tribute to Harriet Tubman*, when I wrote,

> I grew up under the influence of a Bible-believing mother. . . . She believed that God "hath made of one blood all nations of men for to dwell on all the face of the earth" (Acts 17:26 KJV). I learned how to pray from hearing my mother cry out to the Lord. She pleaded with God for all humans to receive Jesus' gift of redemptive love and God's forgiveness.[14]

Christians are expected to share our testimonies of how we received Jesus as Lord and Savior. In Mark 5:19, Jesus instructs his disciples to "go home to your own people and tell them how much the Lord has done for you, and how he has had mercy on you."

When Jeanne DeFazio asked me to do a foreword for her book *The Christian World Liberation Front*, once again, I drew from my personal experiences and wrote,

> I am contributing to this dialogue as an African American to bridge the racial divide. I like the fact that in the 1960s and 1970s, CWLF promoted inclusion, espousing interracial harmony in an era when structural racism was the status quo and "something you're not meant to talk about in public."[15]

I also drew from my personal experiences of teaching to describe CWLF as a model of multicultural communal life.

> We learn best from one another. This is termed "peer learning" in the academic world. CWLF is an excellent model of multicultural communal life. CWLF members from culturally diverse backgrounds lived together and outreached creatively. This teaches millennial readers a valuable lesson.[16]

13. Mathis, *Jesus Among the Homeless*, xiv.
14. Davis and DeFazio, *Artistic Tribute to Harriet Tubman*, 1.
15. DeFazio, *Christian World Liberation Front*, xiii.
16. DeFazio, *Christian World Liberation Front*, xiii.

Further, I identified CWLF as a model of Christian egalitarian leadership.

> David Gill founded New College (CWLF's educational outreach). Sharon Gallagher and Ginny Hearn worked side by side with him in the administration and education of students. I was particularly interested in the advancement of women as administrators and educators in CWLF's New College. Education blurs color lines and creates interracial harmony in the workplace.[17]

Once again, I referenced my experience teaching racially diverse inner city students inclusion.

> In over thirty years teaching racially diverse inner city students, I applied scriptural and constitutional principles developing strategies that empowered students to mobilize and succeed in predominantly white institutions of higher education. So many of these students have acquired professional status and make a difference in their own lives and within their communities.[18]

You have to write about what you know. I explained that CWLF leaders revered Scripture as the word of God.

> The Christian World Liberation Front modeled scripturally-based revival and reform. CWLF members regarded Scripture as "historically accurate, and consistent in itself, fully reliable, and authoritative as God's revelation" (HPA Mission Statement). Jack Sparks held a PhD from the University of Iowa and taught research and design in the educational psychology department at Penn State University and debated with Berkeley intellectuals as an equal; he was also a holy man who esteemed and revered Scripture as the word of God.[19]

Jack Sparks affirmed the reality of hell and the need for repentance from sin. He preached the good news that God forgives all humans through Jesus' innocent shed blood on Calvary.

I concluded my foreword in the CWLF book with a call for repentance and revival in the church in view of Jesus' imminent return:

> In the midst of a pandemic, wildfires, racial violence, and the invasion of Ukraine, there has never been a better time to humble

17. DeFazio, *Christian World Liberation Front*, xiii.

18. DeFazio, *Christian World Liberation Front*, xiii; DeFazio, *Commission*, xi–xii.

19. DeFazio, *Christian World Liberation Front*, xiv.

> ourselves, repent and ask God to forgive us and heal our land (2 Chr 7:14). Repentance will fill our hearts with love for one another and the peace of God, bringing revival and social reform. Twenty-first-century evangelists must give millennials of every color and political inclination the opportunity to receive Jesus as Lord and Savior. CWLF led a colorblind outreach to the secular community. We need to follow in its footsteps.[20]

Brother Curtis Almquist, SSJE, explains, "We have right now the opportunity to make changes in how we live and share life together. How shall we begin?"[21]

It is an honor to share my testimony as an African American in this book. Your published personal testimony based on Scripture will also reach the lost for Jesus:

As Rev 12:11 explains, "And they overcame him by the blood of the Lamb, and by the word of their testimony; and they loved not their lives unto the death."

Julia C. Davis has an EdM from the Harvard Graduate School of Education and an EdM from Bouve College of Health Sciences at Northeastern University. She has held teaching certificates in New York, Massachusetts, and the District of Columbia and has been certified as an assistant principal and as an assistant special education supervisor. Julia has taught in the public and private sector in community-based programs including METCO, Summer STEP opportunities for underrepresented populations in science and technology, and Head Start. She has served as a member of Parent's Advocacy Group for Massachusetts supporting FAPE and mainstreaming special education students. She has taught pre-K through all twelve grades, adult non-readers, limited English language learners, and GED preparation courses. Julia taught internationally as an undergraduate exchange student in a special education program based in Newnham on Severn, Gloucester shire, England, which operated under the auspices of Antioch College in Ohio. Julia and her husband Dan have three children and three grandchildren. They attend the International Family Church in North Reading, Massachusetts.

20. DeFazio, *Christian World Liberation Front*, xiv.

21. Almquist, "Making Meaning," 10; DeFazio, *Christian World Liberation Front*, xiv.

Wilma Faye Mathis

# Chapter Four

# How My Ministry to the Homeless Inspired My Doctoral Dissertation and My Book *Jesus Among the Homeless*

Wilma Faye Mathis

I AM HONORED TO PARTICIPATE in this project. My thanks to Rev. Dr. William David Spencer for including *Jesus Among the Homeless* as recommended reading for the seminar that inspired this book, *The Digital Seminar: Expanding Your Ministry by Writing for Publication.* I am indebted to the Spencers for publishing my doctoral dissertation, *Jesus Among the Homeless*, in their House of Prisca and Aquila series of Wipf and Stock Publishing. I am proud that since its publication, *Jesus Among the Homeless* has been placed in the Library of Congress.

I am going to be honest with you. It was hard work. There were publishing deadlines with Wipf and Stock I had to meet while I worked full-time as a senior project manager at a community health center and conducted my ministry Mom2Mom. The editing issues were complex and challenging. The bibliography alone took hours to edit since some of the online resources included in my dissertation were no longer available by the time Wipf and Stock published the book. I had sleepless nights. I drove out to "Mass and Cass" in Boston and photographed the homeless tents in the city included in the book so that I could meet Wipf and Stock's "permission to publish requirements." It wasn't my first publication but it was the most challenging. And it was worth it. I am grateful for the women who contributed to *Jesus Among the Homeless.* Julia C. Davis, who wrote the foreword, holds an EdM from Harvard Graduate School of Education. Thanks to Julia, the book was featured in *Harvard Magazine*'s Authors' Bookshelf and placed in Harvard Library. In her foreword to this book, Julia reminds us to stand on the word of God. I agree with Julia. I also thank Jeanne DeFazio for her chapter "Building Christian Community For the Homeless," Dr. Martha Reyes for her chapter "The Hosanna Foundation," and Olga Soler for her afterword "Those Without a Home." These contributions gave my book the perfect final touch. In my chapter, "Empowering the Practical Lives of Homeless Women Through Transformational Journaling," I explain that biblical journaling empowers homeless women to take charge of their lives: "Since journaling plays a positive role in aiding recovery from drug addiction, biblical transformational journaling can also play positive roles in helping homeless women."[1] As Julia identifies in her foreword, following scriptural guidelines is the secret to a happy and successful life. Joshua 1:8 explains, "This Book of the Law shall not depart from your mouth, but you shall meditate on it day and night, so that you may be careful to do according to all that is written in it. For then you will make your way prosperous, and then you will have good success."[2]

Why did I volunteer with the homeless while working full-time and getting a doctoral degree? I am a pastor and I have to practice what I preach. "We are instructed to care for widows and orphans (including the homeless)."[3] James 1:27 declares, "Religion that God our Father accepts as pure and spotless is this, to look after orphans and widows in their distress and to keep oneself from being polluted by the world."[4]

I also use digital tools to provide holistic support (emotional, mental, spiritual) through my online ministry Mom2Mom to help people stay connected between in-person moments. I ran the Zoom meeting for "The Digital Evangelist" seminar, sharing the screens, providing technical support so the participants could discuss their publishing goals in breakout rooms, and recorded the seminar session to upload to YouTube. If I can do this, by the grace of God, so can you.

Revelation 14:15 instructs us, "Take your sickle and reap, because the time to reap has come, for the harvest of the earth is ripe."

Wilma Faye Mathis serves as pastor of Manifested Visions Ministries, Inc., Boston, Massachusetts, and the visionary for Mom2Mom, a ministry for single moms and women from all walks of life. Wilma has served the

1. Mathis, *Jesus Among the Homeless*, 67.
2. Mathis, *Jesus Among the Homeless*, xiv.
3. Mathis, *Jesus Among the Homeless*, 79.
4. Mathis, *Jesus Among the Homeless*, xiii.

church in many capacities and is currently the Women's Department vice president in her national organization. Professionally, Wilma is a senior project manager and entrepreneur. She holds a master of arts in urban ministry, a master of divinity from Gordon-Conwell Theological Seminary, and a doctorate in ministry from Knox Theological Seminary, Fort Lauderdale, Florida. She served as teaching assistant in systematic theology at Gordon-Conwell Theological Seminary. Wilma also finds time to volunteer at homeless shelters for women, providing a safe space of encouragement and transformation in the company of Christians. She is an avid Bible scholar and counts it a privilege to teach and preach the word of God. She is a proud mom, loves the Lord, and avails herself to be used for God's glory.

Saideh H. Bonab

# Chapter Five

# Out of the Grip of the Ayatollah, Into the Arms of Jesus

*How My Journey to Jesus Teaches Me About Praying for the Middle East*

**Saideh H. Bonab**

I AM HONORED THAT DRS. Aída Besançon and William David Spencer posted my testimony, "How My Journey to Jesus Teaches Me About Praying for the Middle East" on their blog *Applying Biblical Truths Today*. I participated in the seminar "The Digital Evangelist: Expanding Your Ministry by Writing for Publication," and I am contributing to this book by the same name because my blog was required reading for the seminar. In 2024, I was a student in Dr. William Spencer's Systematic Theology course at Gordon-Conwell Theological Seminary's Center Campus for Urban Ministerial Education in Boston. Jeanne DeFazio, an Athanasian scholar helping students succeed in the class, encouraged me to publish my testimony. She said that my conversion from Islam to Christianity was such a powerful story that many souls would receive Jesus just from reading it. My blog got thousands of views. It was published on the first day of the Iranian and Israeli bombings. I identified how to pray for peace in the Middle East in this blog. We have adapted it for this book:

## How My Journey to Jesus Teaches Me about Praying for the Middle East[1]

Guest blog by Saideh H. Bonab with Jeanne C. DeFazio

How can Christians pray for everyone to bring peace to the Middle East? Jesus' solution was for his followers to help everyone to reconcile with God: "Therefore go and make disciples of all nations, baptizing them in the name of the Father and of the Son and of the Holy Spirit, and teaching them to obey everything I have commanded you. And surely I am with you always, to the very end of the age" (Matt 28:19–20).[2]

My name is Saideh H. Bonab and I am an Iranian Christian and a former student at Gordon-Conwell Theological Seminary, sharing how to pray for everyone to receive Jesus. Once I converted to Christianity, I saw the beauty and the power to change lives of my glorious Lord Jesus, who instilled peace, love, joy in me, and the desire to love and serve others. I knew that I had made the best decision in my life by believing and trusting in him. One core tenet of orthodox Christianity is that the Lord Jesus died on the cross and rose from the dead to atone for the sins of all humans, as Peter, one man whose life Jesus Christ changed, reports, "For Christ also suffered once for sins, the righteous for the unrighteous, to bring you to God. He was put to death in the body but made alive in the Spirit" (1 Pet 3:18).

This is what I experienced: Jesus died for everyone, Christians, Muslims, Jews, Hindus, and Buddhists. Jesus is a living God who has thoughts and emotions and speaks to us and guides us because his Spirit is alive in us. To reach out to a Muslim, I develop a trusting relationship between us. I have compassion for unbelievers looking at them through the lens of love, respect, and humility through the heart of the Lord Jesus, which he opened to me. I don't mock and criticize anyone. I share about my own conversion and change of heart, especially the testimonies of the numerous prayers Jesus has answered as he guides me through my daily life.

I have learned that Jesus is the Prince of Peace and does not believe in an "eye for an eye" and "a tooth for a tooth." In Luke 6:29, Jesus taught, "If someone slaps you on one cheek, turn to them the other also. If someone takes your coat, do not withhold your shirt from them" (Luke 6:29). The

1. This testimony was originally published in *Applying Biblical Truths Today*, June 9, 2025.

2. All Bible quotations are from the NIV 2022.

idea of forgiveness, rather than revenge, is a core message of Christianity. I build a relationship with my Muslim friends with love and respect. Christians must not forget that once we all were in the darkness and the Lord found us and called us to be his hands and feet. So, let us be the light of Jesus in this dark, broken world and bring his light and glory to everyone.

I have found Dr. John Azumah's book *My Neighbour's Faith* helpful when he states that

> Despite the effects of [Muslim] theologians and polemicists over the centuries, and the negative and even hostile news about Jesus that they have produced, many Muslims around the world continue to be fascinated by Jesus. In a survey of over six hundred converts to Christianity from various parts of the world, one in four speaks of the role the figure of Jesus played in their religious development. Many speak of him appearing to them in dreams and visions, sometimes in direct encounters. Their ideas may not be quite clear, but what is clear is that Jesus is encountered as a very real person: a master, a friend, someone who listens to each of them and helps.[3]

As soon as I read this, I got up dancing and crying, realizing that my husband was not the only Muslim who had a personal encounter with the Lord Jesus Christ and received him as his Lord and Savior. Over six hundred others are documented to have had direct encounters and visions with Jesus.

All glory to Jesus! As Christians, we need to testify to the living Christ rather than engaging in fruitless debate of who he is and who he is not. The Lord of lords and King of kings performed so many miracles. These miracles are beyond comprehension. The Lord of glory and majesty cares for the marginalized, widows, the poor, orphans, for everyone from every diaspora, and he is the healer of the sick. I tell everyone who asks me to pray to believe that Jesus is the healer of our sick bodies and souls. Isaiah 53:4 explains, "Surely he took up our pain and bore our suffering" (which Matthew relates to Jesus' healing of the demon-possessed and the sick in Matt 8:16–17). There is no one like Jesus in this entire universe. So, how does prayer impact national and world events? Lisa Schrad explains,

> Prayer transforms us, and our individual transformation does bring change in the world. St. Francis put it even better: "Sanctify yourself and you will sanctify society." It feels so much more

3. Azumah, *My Neighbour's Faith*, 128.

> glamorous and enticing to go sanctify society first, right? I'd much rather work on problems "out there" than have to face my own sin. But how can we even know what true justice and mercy are—much less how we are called to live them out in the world—unless we are first people whose hearts have been changed by God to love those things?[4]

In short, praying for others to change begins with praying for ourselves to change to become the people Jesus wants us to be. Praying for other societies to change follows our prayers and our work in changing our own society to be what Jesus wants it to be. The Great Commission to go into all the world and make disciples by teaching all that Jesus commands starts at home, then reaches out across the world. Our prayers are based on the change Jesus made in us, his filling us with peace, love, and joy.

When I discovered the real Jesus, I mentioned to my Muslim husband that we were not serving the living God. Then he had an encounter with Jesus and fell in love with the Lord. He was so excited to tell me about his encounter that I thought he would live. He was in the hospital dying of cancer. When he died, shortly after, he died in peace going into Jesus' everlasting arms.

Today, one of my two favorite Scriptures is Mark 8:36: "What good is it to gain the whole world and to lose our soul?" The other one is Matt 25:35–36: "I was hungry and you fed me, and I was sick and you looked after me, and I was in prison and you visited me." My husband and I have done these, as we practiced hospitality in our humble home. These days, our family is emotional because my little girl is graduating and is becoming a scientist, just like her father, and cries a lot, missing her father. I told her that her dad is present in spirit. She is getting a dual degree and she also won an award with money, so she is very excited. The good and gracious Lord has been on our side and a beautiful Provider and has given us joy and his peace.

Jesus has been changing our lives. As I learn more and more about the impact of Jesus' death for my failings, I want everyone to benefit from his sacrifice. I want everyone of every faith to discover Jesus is a living God, whose compassion and love is gracious and kind and brings light to our darkness, just as he brought light to my life and the lives of those I love by his great love and care.

4. Schrad, "What Difference Does Prayer Make," para. 6.

This was a very emotional time for me. I was praying for my family in Iran because I could not get through to them by telephone. I wanted to hear their voices and tell them I loved them and was praying for them. It was a heartbreaking time but God used my story to touch people's hearts for Jesus. Jesus was there for me every step of the way. Holding me close to Him. He wants to be there for you in times of trouble. Let Him inside your heart. He is the Lover of your soul.[5]

I want to close by sharing this beautiful poem by Terry McDermott:

## About to Pass By

Close your eyes so you can see,
Quiet your mind and let it be.
A silent place so you can hear,
The One and Only will draw near.
Slowly look beyond yourself,
Place your fears upon the shelf.
Gently breathe, play your part,
Time to listen to your heart.
A gentle whisper, a sunshine ray,
I love you more than words can say.
Turn to Me when others turn away,
Believe Me forever and a day.[6]

Saideh Bonab left her homeland in Persia at seventeen to study Dante Alighieri in Italy. She holds a degree from the University in Perugia and is fluent in five languages and one dialect. Saideh prayed for the Lord to bring her a husband. The answer to her prayer was a marriage to the love of her life, a distinguished Iranian-born medical physicist, scientist and radiologist. The product of that love is her beautiful daughter, whom she loves very much and is extremely proud of. While dying of cancer, her beloved

5. Saideh H. Bonab granted permission via text for her photo and text to be included in this book, July 9, 2025.

6. Terry McDermott granted permission via email for his poem to be included in this book, July 18, 2025.

husband had an encounter with the glorious, divine Lord Jesus. This experience led her family to convert from Islam to Christianity. She completed a bachelor's degree in nursing from the University of Massachusetts. After the passing of her husband, she became a geriatric and pediatric nurse and has worked in flu clinics and as a public school nurse. In the fall of 2025, she completed her master of arts in Christian ministries degree at Gordon-Conwell Theological Seminary's Boston Center for Urban Ministerial Education. She currently attends Grace Chapel in Lexington, Massachusetts, where she works with the homeless. She looks forward to working for God bringing in the end-time harvest. In her own words, "My goal and mission is to bring the good news of my Lord of lords and King of kings to the lost and hurting. To reach the poor and marginalized so they understand that there is no one like him and that he is the global God for Jews, Christians, Hindus, Muslims, and Buddhists."

Dr. Ted Baehr

# Chapter Six

# How the Movie Guide Founder Discovered the Big Picture

Ted Baehr

In 1975, God rescued me from the bondage to sin. I had begun financing independent movies for Canon Films when an older friend, who had come to know Jesus Christ at the Billy Graham Crusade in New York City in 1957, suggested that I read the Bible to show her what was wrong with it. Reading God's word in order to refute it changed my perspective both professionally and personally. God rescued me. Suddenly, life made sense. Chasing after empty promises lost its appeal. Hedonism relinquished its hold on me by God's grace alone. There was no withdrawal from stopping the addictions, only the peace that comes from a personal encounter with Jesus Christ. Immediately, I was compelled to marry my beloved. The week before the wedding, a friend asked me if I wanted to accept Jesus Christ as my Lord and Savior and be filled with his Holy Spirit. I did. Filled with the Holy Spirit through my new faith in Jesus Christ, I decided to attend seminary at the Institute of Theology at the Cathedral of St. John the Divine.[1]

"Millard Robert E. Theodore Baehr (born 1946) is an American media critic and chairman of . . . Good News Communications, Inc. He is publisher and editor-in-chief of Movieguide, a website and biweekly journal that evaluates motion pictures and other entertainment products from a Christian perspective on suitability for family consumption. He also hosts nationally and internationally syndicated Movieguide radio and television programs. . . . Baehr graduated summa cum laude in comparative literature and as a Rufus Choate Scholar from Dartmouth College. He then received

1. Reprinted from DeFazio and Spencer, *Redeeming the Screens*, 5: Ted Baehr granted permission via email for his photo and text to be included in this book, Feb. 6, 2026.

a Juris Doctor from New York University School of Law . . . and received his Doctor of Humanities degree from Belhaven College"[2] and a doctor of theology degree from Primus University of Theology. He is the author of *How to Succeed in Hollywood (Without Losing Your Soul): A Fieldguide for Christian Screenwriters, Actors, Producers, Directors, and More.*

2. Wikipedia, "Ted Baehr," paras. 1, 3, 4.

Susan Stafford

# Chapter Seven

# Our Eternal Chapter Begins on Earth

### Susan Stafford

At thirteen, I had gone to the Billy Graham Crusade in Kansas City on a Baptist church bus trip. I took my walk up the aisle and gave my life to the Lord. More than twenty years later, I was a syndicated radio broadcaster with the McLendon radio stations and interviewed Hal Lindsey, author of *The Late Great Planet Earth*. Hal suggested I find a church, so I began attending Pastor Jack Hayford's Church on the Way. As an adult, and understanding more about the Lord, I recommitted my life to him on May 7, 1972.

I began hosting Bible studies in my home for Rev. Kenn Gulliksen, which evolved into what is now the Vineyard. This was my introduction to born-again Christians (Gavin and Patti MacLeod, Pat and Shirley Boone, Billy Davis Jr. and Marilyn McCoo) who have become lifelong friends. Rev. Bob Reith of Media Fellowship International baptized me in the Jordan River in the early 1980s. . . . I lived a life of self, and my "self" died. God placed a call on my life, and I have found great satisfaction in serving the Lord Jesus Christ. Life on earth is, in essence, an introduction to eternity. When we do not know Jesus, we make choices as though there is no afterlife. In reality, how we live in this life determines our eternal state. I understand from personal experience that earthly accomplishments have no value in my gaining eternal life. My highest social or civic honors will not earn me entrance into heaven. Speaking from personal experience, I often explain what it is like as a Christian to take up my cross daily and follow the saints who have preceded me.

I mentioned that my childhood left me with abandonment issues that took a lifetime to work out. I have learned to view life from an eternal perspective and find value because I am loved and accepted in my beloved

Jesus, whose love has brought the greatest emotional healing in my life. The experience of being accepted in the Beloved, which Paul expresses in Eph 1:6, reminds me constantly of the wonderful kindness God has poured out on me because I belong to his dearly loved Son, Jesus. God brought me into unmerited favor through Jesus' death and resurrection and made me the object of his grace and mercy.[1]

"Susan Stafford is an American former model, actress, and television host. She was the original daytime hostess of the American game show *Wheel of Fortune* from January 6, 1975, until she left on October 22, 1982."[2] Susan Stafford is the author of *Stop the Wheel, I Want to Get Off*, coeditor with Jeanne C. DeFazio of *Media Fellowship International*, and a contributing author to *Redeeming the Screens*, *The Commission*, and *The Journey Home.*

1. Reprinted from DeFazio, *Journey Home*, 12–14; Susan Stafford granted permission via phone for her photo and text to be included in this book, July 19, 2025.

2. Wikipedia, "Susan Stafford," para. 1.

Mel Novak

# Chapter Eight

# A Mother's Faith Blesses Her Son

## Mel Novak

I WAS BLESSED WITH A praying Christian mother. When I was a child, the medical prognosis was that my leg would have to be amputated. Through the prayers of my mother, God miraculously healed my leg. Her faith influenced my life deeply. My faith in God grew as I experienced a series of injuries that were miraculously healed. A native of Pittsburgh, Pennsylvania, I was an outstanding athlete in several sports who passed up sixty football scholarship offers to sign a pro-baseball contract with the Pittsburgh Pirates. My career was cut short by a massive rotator cuff tear. Through prayer and very challenging rehabilitation therapy, my rotator cuff tear healed. I endured ten failed surgeries on my throat in ten years, and, once again, the example of my mother's deep faith and prayers encouraged mine, resulting in each miraculous healing. I look back now and realize that, through every infirmity, God gave me healing after healing that encouraged my faith in him.[1]

"Milan Mrdjenovich (Serbian: Милан Мрђеновић, Milan Mrđenović; June 16, 1934 – April 9, 2025), known as Mel Novak, was an American actor who was best known for villainous roles in *Black Belt Jones*, *Game of Death*, and *An Eye for an Eye*. He was also known for doing all of his own stunts and fighting scenes. . . . Novak was also an ordained minister, known for doing celebrity funerals and memorials for the likes of Chuck Connors' son, Jeffrey Alan Connors, and Tim Burton's father, Bill Burton. He worked in skid row and prison ministry for over 39 years."[2]

1. Photo and text reprinted from DeFazio and Spencer, *Redeeming the Screens*, 74.
2. Wikipedia, "Mel Novak," para. 1, 5.

We are grateful for Mel Novak's permission to include him in *Creative Ways to Build Christian Community*, *Redeeming the Screens*, *The Commission*, and *The Journey Home* so that we are able to quote him in this book.

Jeanne's personal note, written prior to Mel's passing: "Mel Novak's ministry, Heavenly Manna Inc., has greatly impacted my life. Mel is a dedicated soldier of Christ, an ordained minister called by God to share the Good News of salvation in Jesus Christ with the homeless on skid row and in the prisons. He reaches out to those that many people did not want to have anything to do with. His ministry is unique in that it built Christian community among the helpless and hopeless: those who have nothing and no one. For the past thirty years, Mel has faithfully ministered at Los Angeles rescue missions, and for the past twenty-seven years, he has also ministered in penitentiaries nationwide. Through Mel's ministry, thousands have accepted God's precious gift of salvation through grace, by receiving Jesus Christ as their Lord and Savior or rededicating their lives to Jesus. Mel's deliverance and protection prayers built Christian community within the walls of penal institutions and among the homeless."[3]

3. Reprinted from DeFazio and Lathrop, *Creative Ways*, 13.

Jeanne DeFazio, Bob Yerkes, and LeaAnn Pendergrass[4]

4. Bob Yerkes, honored by the Stuntmen's Association with a Lifetime Achievement Award; LeaAnn Pendergrass granted permission for this photo to be included in this book, July 23, 2025.

# Chapter Nine

# A Legendary Stuntman Reveals How He Was Mentored by the Greatest "High Work Performer" of All Times

**Bob Yerkes**

Top Hollywood stuntman Bob Yerkes shared his Christian testimony in *Redeeming the Screens*:

> While with Ringling Brothers Circus, I decided to read the Bible. I grew up with a blind Christian aunt who possessed great spiritual insight, and her belief in Jesus impacted my early life, though I was reared in an unbelieving home. As a young adult, I have to confess I read the Bible planning to denounce the truth of it, but I realized that it had to be inspired by God. Steve Terrell, the oldest son in the television series *Life with Father*, took me to the Village Church in Burbank, California. At twenty-five years old, I became a believer. I formed a group at Ringling Brothers Circus to read and study the Bible. I got my two friends, Reggie Armour and Bill Snyder, interested, and the first Bible study meeting was held in Little Rock, Arkansas. The group was nondenominational, including Roman Catholics as well as Protestants. My pastor, Reverend Phil Gibson, sent literature to help us in our worship.[1]

"My motivation for ministry to the media could be summed up like this: I was mentored by the world's greatest stuntman who specialized in high work. His name was Jesus Christ. He stood in for everyone up on the cross. And he sustains me by his Spirit."[2]

Jeanne's editorial note: I am grateful that Bob Yerkes contributed to *Creative Ways to Build Christian Community*, *Redeeming the Screens*, *The*

1. DeFazio and Spencer, *Redeeming the Screens*, 57.
2. DeFazio and Stafford, *Media Fellowship International*, 12.

*Commission*, and *The Journey Home* so that I am able to quote him in this book. I will never forget the time he took me to a circus tent and stopped to share his faith with a trapeze artist. His heart was so great to reach the lost for Jesus. . . . The New York Times eulogized Bob Yerkes as a legend in the circus and stunt world and a devout Christian.[3]

"Brayton Walter Yerkes (February 11, 1932 – October 1, 2024), known professionally as Bob Yerkes, was an American stuntman."[4] He received the World Acrobatics Society's Lifetime Achievement Award, the Taurus Works Stuntman Award and the Remo Williams Award for his best high work dangling from the Statue of Liberty with no net below him. The Bob Yerkes Award is presented at the Annual Icon Award Ceremony. He provided free training and equipment for Hollywood's action stars in his backyard.

3. Reprinted from DeFazio and Stafford, *Media Fellowship International*, 14; see also, Rosenwald, "Bob Yerkes."

4. Wikipedia, "Bob Yerkes," para. 1.

Gemma Wenger on *Beauty For Ashes*

# Chapter Ten

# A Father's Love Is One of God's Greatest Presents

Gemma Wenger

I was born to Raymond John Wenger Jr., a brilliant Harvard Law School graduate who had a heart to become a priest. When the priesthood did not materialize, he instead married a Protestant woman from Kansas, Beulah "Bee" Beyer. Beulah had left the Midwest for California to be with my father and eventually became a celebrity cooking show television host. Through various real-estate investments, my parents were finally able to purchase a modest home in a nice neighborhood in Los Angeles. From a young age, I was groomed by God. My father, being a godly man, led me to the Lord when I was three years old with the promise that "presents" would ensue. He encouraged my sister, Lisa, and me to pray for an hour a day, and he, being Catholic, faithfully took us to daily Mass. I remember my sister and me lying with my dad on the big king-sized master bed with the gigantic orange velvet comforter and him telling us all about Jesus. He said that, if we asked Jesus into our hearts, then we would get presents. I said, "Oh, yes, I want that." My father led me in the sinner's prayer, and I remember the feeling I had at such a young age when Jesus came into my heart. I specifically remember asking my dad,"Where are the presents?" My dad responded, "They are coming, you will see. They don't come all at one time, but they will be here." I remember having a feeling of disappointment at not having actual presents, but God gave me a vision of presents in my head. I saw them in the Spirit. I can still see that exact same vision in my mind today that I had many years ago. I have seen the gifts of God in my life, and I do praise God for all of his miraculous wonders that he has done throughout the years.[1]

1. Reprinted from DeFazio and Spencer, *Redeeming the Screens*, 116–17; Gemma

"Gemma Wenger is a Christian pastor, interview show producer/host, singer/songwriter, and author. She is the producer/host for *Gemma Wenger's Hollywood* and *Beauty for Ashes* which were Official Selections in the 2021 International Christian Film & Music Festival. She is the songwriter for 'Trust' as well having been a contributing author to multiple books."[2]

---

Wenger granted permission via email for her photo and text to be included in this book, July 11, 2025.

2. Wikipedia, "Gemma Wenger," para. 1.

Jozy Pollock[3]

3. Jozy Pollock granted permission via email for her photo and text to be included in this book, July 11, 2025; see also, Taogaga, "On Faith Alone Jozy Pollock."

# Chapter Eleven

# Visible to the Liberating God, Invisible to Predatory Men

**Jozy Pollock**

In 1982, a relationship I had with a man I had found through a psychic's predictions brought me to the end of my rope. I called a friend named Mike who had accepted Jesus after years of drinking and drugging. I told him that I had had enough torment and I wanted peace. He told me that, if I prayed the sinner's prayer, I could have peace. I did not feel like a sinner, because I had always been a good friend and looked out for others. I was the unpaid psychiatrist to my friends who were going through traumas. I prayed the sinner's prayer, but pleaded with the Lord not to turn me into a Jesus freak. I went to a Chi Coltrane Christian concert at the Vineyard. She was talking about being "born again," explaining that it was a step of faith, and that salvation is assured even if you are not feeling it. This was exactly where I was in my walk. I found out she had a Bible study at her home, and I attended. I told her how I was feeling. She prayed with me and laid hands on me. I started speaking in tongues. Suddenly, I had a huge hunger and thirst for God. It took me a long time to submit to the Holy Spirit, but, after I gave up my will, I had peace. When I was water baptized in a home in Bel Air, I fell in love with Jesus and became invisible to men. I needed to build my relationship with Jesus. I have been celibate since being saved. This was God's shield.[1]

"Jozy Pollock is an actress, songwriter, and Christian minister for prisons. She was born in 1935 in the United Kingdom. She is the author of *Backstage Pass to Heaven* (2017), a book which is a story of a Jetsetter, Jozy Pollock, who went from hanging out with the rich and famous for ministering to

1. Reprinted from DeFazio and Spencer, *Redeeming the Screens*, 66–67.

the notorious in the penal system. She was Britain's hula hoop queen, but her career came to a halt when she married the famous magician Channing Pollock. She appeared on the Ed Sullivan Show and performed in Las Vegas as Channing's assistant. After accepting Jesus as Lord and Savior, Jozy gave up a life of glamour and volunteered with the prison chaplaincy services at East Lake Juvenile Hall in downtown Los Angeles. She became the first Protestant female chaplain at Los Angeles Men's Central Jail. Noelle Aimee Kozell directed a documentary about Jozy's twenty years in prison ministry entitled *On Faith Alone: The Jozy Pollock Story*. Throughout her life, she has met and befriended celebrities and understands from personal experience that many celebrities do not have the peace and love that comes from having a personal relationship with God."[2]

2. WikiChristian, "Jozy Pollock," para. 1–7.

Richard Bruce

# Chapter Twelve

# It Was in the Cards

## Richard Bruce

My parents are agnostics, but they are very active in their Protestant church. I, like my parents, enjoyed church activities but still considered myself an agnostic. While I was a graduate student in economics, a number of coincidences and the help of my Evangelical Protestant neighbors encouraged me to reconsider. I became a believing Christian, but I still had to choose a church. The only options I took seriously were Evangelical Protestantism and Catholicism. I prayed, fasted, and studied both theology and history. I knew the evidence favored the Catholic Church, but I wanted to be very sure. As the Protestants based their claims on the Bible, I decided to do an intensive study of the New Testament. Starting with Matthew, I wrote down relevant passages on three-by-five cards. There were some isolated verses that seemed to support Protestant doctrines, though they could also be explained in a Catholic manner. On the other hand, there was a large stack of cards that supported Catholic doctrine, and many of them were difficult or impossible to explain in Protestant terms. Three-quarters of the way through the New Testament, I had a stack of cards about two-and-a-half inches thick and I felt the evidence was sufficiently overwhelming. So instead of writing the passages in the last part of the New Testament, I underlined them. Having finished my careful study of doctrine, history, and, most of all, the Bible, I acted on the results and was received into the Catholic Church.[1]

Richard Bruce has a BA, MA, and PhC (ABD), in economics from the University of California and is a former full-time economics instructor

1. Richard Bruce granted permission via phone for his photo and text to be included in this book from Bruce, "It Was in the Cards."

at St. John's University. "Including the secular publications, he has published twenty-five articles in all [most notably] 'A Possible Solution to the Vouchers Issue,' in *New Oxford Review*, a controversial Catholic intellectual magazine."[2]

2. See "Personal Website of Richard Lee Bruce": https://richleebruce.com; and Bruce, "Possible Solution."

Terry McDermott

# Chapter Thirteen

# The Power of the Poem

Terry McDermott

I WROTE THE ENCLOSED POEM in remembrance of the six million Jews killed in the Holocaust. I chose the title "The Shoes of Auschwitz" because Auschwitz is a symbol of terror and genocide, which is anti-Semitism at its worst. The closing of this poem offers a personal relationship with Jesus as the spiritual solution to every human atrocity because Jesus is the Jew and the Son of God who redeems humankind and restores our rightful relationship to God the Father:

### "The Shoes of Auschwitz"

Stopped dead in my tracks,
When confronted with the facts.
Thousands of shoes piled high,
Tombstones for those who did not have to die.
The voice of suffering,
No buffering.
Eighty years later, bodies still piled high,
The American holocaust as our children die.
Can you smell that smell,
Satan dancing in the fires of hell?
Before another child falls,
Tear down the walls.

I wonder what they would say,
Morality up and walked away.
Look what is in store,
Blood on the floor.
Let the trumpets sound,
As the walls fall to the ground.
A child will never see a new dawn,
All her tomorrows are gone.
From the North African city of Carthage,
Children burned, envision the carnage.
To Germany, shoes with no laces,
Now, American children with no faces.
Decimation for all to see,
Never, ever let it be.
Only hope to end the strife,
Turn to the Bread of Life.
The epitome of love,
Rending the heavens from above.
The One many people never knew.
Jesus is a Jew.[1]

Terry McDermott holds a BA from Santa Clara University; a JD from the University of California, Davis, School of Law; and an LLM from the University of California, Berkeley, School of Law. He is a lecturer in law, emeritus, Sacramento State University.

1. Reprinted from Mann, *Otto and the White Dove*, x–xi.

Aaron Ezra Mann[2]

2. Aaron Mann was interviewed by Sid Roth on his program *It's Supernatural.* The interview was taped on Oct. 9, 2025, and featured Ezra Mann as a Holocaust survivor and an Academy Award winner. See "Sid Roth's It's Supernatural": https:www.sidroth.org.

# Chapter Fourteen

# The Power in the Play

Aaron Ezra Mann

JEANNE'S EDITORIAL NOTE: AARON Ezra Mann participates in this project to share his testimony. The recent photos of malnourished children in Gaza City have been a stark reminder of Nazi Germany for him. His family experienced starvation during the Holocaust and escaped from Germany to live briefly in Israel and settled in the United States of America. He relates to those suffering in the Middle East and prays for a peaceful resolution. In the foreword of his latest book, Otto and the White Dove,Terry McDermott explains why he wrote the poem "The Shoes of Auschwitz." To paraphrase Terry McDermott's words, Aaron's personal relationship with Jesus is the spiritual solution to every human atrocity he has survived. Jesus is the Jew, and the Son of God, who redeems humankind and restores our rightful relationship to God the Father. Aaron received Jesus in his heart as Lord and Savior and thanks Jesus everyday for his mercy and love that sustains him. Paul, in Rom 2:10, explains that "glory, honor and peace [are available] for everyone who does good: first for the Jew, then for the Gentile."

German-born American producer, writer, and director Aaron "Ezra" Mann is most probably best known for co-producing *In the Region of Ice*. This film won an Academy Award (Oscar) for best short live action drama of 1977.[1]

> Academy Award winning producer Aaron Mann (aka Ezra Mann) was reared in an Orthodox Jewish tradition. His parents were Holocaust survivors. He is acknowledged in *Berkeley Street Theatre* for making a courageous paradigm cultural shift in the Hollywood community by accepting Jesus as Messiah Lord and Savior. His powerful play, *Otto & The White Dove*, is an autobiographical account of his conversion. In it, the White Dove (a manifestation of

1. Mann, *Otto & The White Dove*, 49.

the Holy Spirit) expounds the word of God and brings Otto, a Holocaust survivor, to Jesus. Aaron identifies his life changing experience as he broke Orthodox Hebrew tradition through the power of the Holy Spirit to encounter the risen Jesus in Hollywood's evangelistic Christian communities. Along with Susan Stafford, Patti Zuckor, Gavin and Patti MacLeod, LeaAnn Pendergrass and Linda Chapman, Aaron prays for and ministers God's word to Jewish and Gentile members of the entertainment industry.[2]

2. Spencer and Spencer, *Christian Egalitarian Leadership*, 124.

Linda Lockhart

# Chapter Fifteen

# Surprised by Jesus

Linda Lockhart

IT WAS AN HONOR to participate in "The Digital Evangelist" seminar. I am glad for this opportunity to share my testimony in this book! Years ago, I received God's clarion call. He said, through a pastor, that I was going to be his "mobile unit." I had no clue what was being said to me. As I grew spiritually, I understood that God calls all Christians to step up to the plate. God put Paul's words to Timothy in my heart: "I am giving you this command, in keeping with the prophecies once made about you, so that by recalling them you may fight the battle well (1 Tim 1:18)." I had received a prophecy to be an evangelist. In Eph 4:11–13, Paul identifies the five-fold ministry:

> So Christ himself gave the apostles, the prophets, the evangelists, the pastors and teachers to equip his people for works of service, so that the body of Christ might be built up until we all reach unity in the faith and the knowledge of the son of God and become mature, attaining to the full measure of the fullness of Christ.

Reaching unity in the faith is God's will for the body of Christ in these racially divided times. Martin Luther King Jr. famously said that eleven o'clock on Sunday morning is "the most segregated hour of the week."[1] This statement pointed to the fact that churches in the United States remain largely divided by race. I am Cape Verdean by descent. God has called me to be a digital evangelist that stands for inclusion against structural racism. This is why I published a review of *An Artistic Tribute to Harriet Tubman* in the *Africanus Journal*,[2] and I shared my testimony in *Jesus Among the Homeless*, *The Journey Home*, and *The Commission*.

1. Burge, "Fifty Years After MLK," para. 1.
2. Lockhart, "Review of *An Artistic Tribute*."

If God calls you to publish your testimony or to share it in a panel discussion, please obey him! Revelation 12:11 states, "We overcome by the blood of the Lamb and the word of our testimony." Christians triumph through Jesus' sacrificial death and sharing our stories of faith as God works in our lives. We must take our marching orders from God, in the name of Jesus, seriously! When we stand before God, he will ask, "Did you obey me?" We want to hear him say, "Well done, good and faithful servant, you have been faithful with a few things; I will put you in charge of many things" (Matt 25:21).[3]

Linda Lockhart is a mixed-race mother of Cape Verdean descent and a proactive grandmother and great grandmother of multicultural children as well as a former supervisor for Anchorage Boys Home in Beverly, Massachusetts. She has experience teaching art activities for therapeutic benefit to multiracial at-risk youth in various programs.

3. Linda Lockhart granted permission via text for her photo and personal testimony to be included in this book, Oct. 15, 2025.

William David Spencer and Aida Besançon Spencer

# Chapter Sixteen

# Reaching for the Cities of Refuge

William David Spencer

## Plainfield and North Plainfield in New Jersey

I WAS BORN AND REARED in a church and home that taught a high view of the Bible and of the Trinity. I have treasured this gift throughout my life. My direction-changing encounter with God occurred after an InterVarsity (IVCF) meeting at Rutgers and Douglass colleges, where I and my future wife, Aída Besançon, were both students. I recognized these IVCF students were different from anyone I had met before. Jim VanDuzer explained to me the same gospel teaching with which I had grown up, but this time, I felt like a great golden goblet was poured into my head and plateaued in the middle of my being, and there it has remained, giving me peace in all the tumult life has inflicted. That summer, I stood on my parents' front porch, listening to the National Guard shooting out the streetlights so they would not be targets, as a riot broke out in my birth city of Plainfield, New Jersey. The next day, I learned a policeman had been stomped to death by a mob. I was shocked. I had ridden in these streets on my bike all through my youth and had never perceived such estrangement was seething there. I was a teenager, just starting college and didn't know how to respond, so I did it in the only way I knew—I went out into the center of the city, evangelizing on the street by handing out tracts. One night, two saints from a messianic Jewish ministry in Plainfield saw me handing out Moody Bible Institute science tracts, talking to street people about Jesus, and they invited me to open up their reading room as a contact center on weekend nights. I invited a brilliant friend, who was also a student at Rutgers and whom I had the privilege to lead to the Lord (today, the renowned medievalist Dr. Robert

Boenig, author of the amazingly informative and award-winning book *C. S. Lewis and the Middle Ages*), and we began writing original music on our guitars to attract visitors, though both of us were gentiles. This ministry expanded my hyper-conservative background's view of Christian outreach, and one ministry soon led to another. Forming a Jesus band in 1966, which we called the Spheres (after a reference to "the music of the spheres" in the hymn "This Is My Father's World"), I and David G. K. Howe (now a pastor) and Bob continued writing songs and performing with friends from college, including David Rowe (who became a college chaplain); eventually, Aída and Rick Burton and decorated returning Vietnam war medic Bruce I. McDaniel (today a writer, who, along with his provocative science fiction tales, has recorded his military experiences, in such books as the insightful The Hardest Part: Homecoming Stories from the Vietnam War) replaced the graduates, and with Bob, we continued in seminary, playing our songs honoring the Lord up and down the USA's eastern seacoast for seven years altogether.

## Newark, NJ

In the summer of 1970, I joined the street minister William T. (Bill) Iverson in a program fueled by the financial support of opera singer Jerome Hines to co-run an interracial evangelistic band for Cross Counter ministry in conjunction with Peter Jones, the eventually noted apologist, his future wife, Rebecca Clowney, and her sister, whom I only knew as "Twiz" (but I'm guessing she is Anne in her father's bios), who were wonderful Christians and the daughters of Dr. Edmund Clowney, the president of Westminster Theological Seminary, and Myrtle and Charles Jones (unrelated to Peter). Our job was to make a joyful noise and attract the neighbors (some still in hiding) out of their homes to relate to each local storefront church in huge neighborhood block parties Bill would set up around Newark. Bill Iverson remains the best street preacher I have ever heard. There was always plenty to eat and the gospel message was powerfully shared. Our band, called The Genesis (unrelated to the popular band by the same name, which began at a British school c. 1967), would play and, if the neighborhood had a band, it would play, too. Myrtle had an amazing voice and went on to become a professional singer. We also played music in neighborhoods and parks, once in New York, once on local radio. And during the week, we taught a daily vacation Bible school and ran a coffee house in a Lutheran church just off burned-up-by-the-Newark-riots Springfield Avenue. It was a full and rich ministry experience.

## Philadelphia, PA

After graduation from Rutgers in 1969, I had become a student at Temple University's seminary, which had left the Temple campus to become independent as the Conwell School of Theology in Philadelphia. Aída had been working for Community Action Program as Plainfield's Spanish community organizer. Hearing about all the exciting things I was learning about the Lord and feeling increasingly frustrated, and convinced that she could enrich people's lives more fully by teaching them the truths of the New Testament rather than simply helping them become middle class, she enrolled in Conwell as well. We loved the school. When Conwell closed and moved up north, having merged with Gordon Divinity School, we switched to Princeton under the guidance of the presbytery of Elizabeth, with which we were both now under care. The great textual critic Bruce Metzger was my faculty advisor, and missionary Christy Wilson, just back home from Afghanistan, was our dorm advisor. Christy used to come to the prayer meeting, which Bob and I held in our room, and sit on the floor with us and Aída and anyone who joined us.

## Back to Philadelphia, PA

In the summer after my graduation, while Aída was still studying at Princeton Seminary, I signed up for an arduous ministry in West Philadelphia, attempting to ease racial tension by setting up block associations and Bible studies. It was very poorly planned by a retired army chaplain, who put a hurricane fence around the church and set two vicious guard dogs to patrol the parking lot. At dawn, he would kick me and the only other participant to show up out of the Sunday school building, where we slept on cots, lock up the doors, leave out the dogs, and not let us back in until around 9:00 o'clock at night. A team from the church was supposed to be involved, but only one young student from Westminster Seminary, unrelated to the church, Herb Greenspan, showed up. Herb became a wonderful friend and a blessing to me. We were required to do all the plans the team was supposed to handle. We were getting $6 a week from the church for food and a stipend at the end from the presbytery of Philadelphia. When the pastor discovered the stipend, he cut off the $6. We were supposed to be setting up block associations to solve the racial problems of the neighborhood and then turn these block association meetings into Bible studies. Instead, we discovered a Jehovah's Witnesses' abandoned Bible study. (They were too terrified to return after a gang called the Breed, which occupied a house directly across the street from the church we were trying to serve, stomped a youth to death a month before we arrived). We took over the Bible study and leaped ahead on the plan. The pastor was furious and told us to stick to the plan.

We were hungry and exhausted and this debacle of a ministry triggered a latent intestinal condition in me that became chronic. Herb tried to take care of me and do all the work himself, but when I began to bleed internally, I called up my supervisor and had him drive me back to Princeton Hospital. I was subsequently, over the next decade, hospitalized seven times for this condition, diagnosed as Crohn's disease. Eventually, my doctor advised me to change my street ministering lifestyle or become an invalid.

## Trenton, NJ

A lover of books and a prolific writer since childhood, I had previously, providentially, parlayed a student internship into becoming a part-time position as Protestant Chaplain at Rider College (now University), and now I was hoping it could help me slow down the disease and become more academic. I discovered college ministry is very relational and, therefore, all-consuming, but, I found I loved pastoring college students, including writing sermons to help them grow in Christ. God also gave me the greatest gift of love in my life after the incomparable blessing of my salvation: In 1972, Rev. Bill Iverson presided over my marriage to Aída at Princeton Theological Seminary chapel. Aída, who had worked for Model Cities in Newark and taught English as a second language (ESL) in Perth Amboy, now took a position at Trenton State's maximum security prison. While teaching ESL to Hispanic inmates, she offered them the possibility of having a Bible study or her bringing in Hispanic churches on Sundays. They begged her to do both. I went in with her for the Bible studies and we did this for several years, teaching the Bible to the Hispanic inmates, while she recruited three Spanish churches, Pentecostal, Methodist, and Roman Catholic, to come in to hold services on the weekends. The inmates loved having women come in as volunteers; it helped them feel normal, and they were very protective of their volunteers. Once, an argument was taking place between two inmates on another floor and the Latin inmates began moderating it and guarded the volunteers until the incident was quelled. In our final year, the churches and the inmates held a talent show with the churches providing the food and the inmates singing and performing in what was a joyful and heartrending evening, where the Lord was honored amidst soulful renditions of "Papa Was a Rolling Stone," a Motown song that spoke to countless inmates. Then, suddenly, to my surprise, the Protestant chaplain at a neighboring school, Trenton State College (today The College of New Jersey [TCNJ]), was fired by the president of the school, a devout Christian who was furious at my employer, United Ministries for Higher Education, since this turned out to be the second chaplain in a row who had been preying on the female students. The president threatened to kick the ministries group out, as incompetent to pick a moral chaplain, to find his own Protestant chaplain. The local ministers who comprised the group were abashed, so I suggested they needed a paradigm shift. They had tried two males who had failed miserably. They needed a woman. And I knew a perfect one, with a seminary degree and much professional experience working with people, to recommend: my wife! So, Aída became the Protestant chaplain of Trenton State College and, as always, did a fabulous job. She even brought in inmates from Trenton State Prison, who had become Christians, to speak to appropriate classes and to the Christian student groups. Before and after this wonderful ministry, working with college-age students during the Jesus Movement, we completed our MDiv and ThM degrees at Princeton Theological Seminary.

## Back to Newark, NJ

A year or two later, when the now strapped-for-cash United Ministries for Higher Education was forced to terminate all of its sixteen New Jersey chaplaincies except its four eldest chaplains (who grabbed all the money that was left and had the organization cut the other twelve of us loose), we were invited by Bill Iverson back to Newark to train seminarians in city ministry for Dr. George W. (Bill) Webber's innovative New York Theological Seminary (NYTS) Urban Year program. Bill Iverson was also working together with The Salvation Army's Newark Central Corps in cooperation with Captains Lionel and Marilyn Chapman. Between 1974 to 1978, we taught the NYTS introductory New Testament exegesis class, living in community with our seminarians in a three-story brownstone that had been given to The Salvation Army. Located in the center of Newark, right next to The Salvation Army's central corps, the brownstone was near Newark's three largest colleges. With advice and a gift of paint from Sherwin Williams, we, with our seminarians, invested ten months of scraping, caulking, repairing, and painting in-between classes, and we supervised their ministries while refurbishing this beautiful structure. We named it Alaythia ("truth" in Greek) House and it became a center of ministry, a refuge in the city. Aída and I, with our director Bill Iverson, taught a variety of courses to our seminarians. During that time, local college students began to visit and I gave a well-attended lecture at the New Jersey Institute of Technology on the validity of Jesus' death and resurrection. Also, Aída and I advised the IVCF and Campus Crusade students (Cru) as well as started a campus ministry for The Salvation Army.

When local storefront pastors began to attend our classes, we spun off a college-level program for them and their interested parishioners who did not have college degrees. With Aída as our dean, setting the curriculum, and I as the director of personnel, hiring and (in one case, firing) our teachers, we named it the Alpha-Omega Community Theological School (ACTS) and it soon expanded to two centers in Newark, one more in Jersey City, and another one in the Bedford Stuyvesant Fulton Street area of New York City. This satellite ministry was done in conjunction with Dr. Bob Cook's The King's College, who provided its accreditation, as NYTS had provided the seminary-level accreditation. The ministry was going very well and we were attracting local seminary-trained pastors to teach for us. Among the most exciting for us, Aída and I were teaching the storefront pastors how to read the Greek New Testament, so they could enrich their sermons from the original text.

When The Salvation Army decided to move out of Newark and tear down its buildings, including Alaythia House, the Chapmans, whom we had come to love as our brother and sister, were reassigned to the New Jersey shore. Both Bill Webber and Bill Iverson left the area. Just before all these desertions, Aída and I had encountered a small, struggling Christian college, just overlooking Newark, whose faculty attended the Evangelical Theological Society (ETS), which Aída and I had both joined in 1974. We ran a conference featuring John Montgomery as the speaker at the church affiliated with the school and, noting the school was waning, offered to come alongside so it could work together with ACTS, which had now grown to fifteen faculty and one hundred-plus students. Instead of pursuing the partnership idea, the school filed a complaint with the New Jersey accrediting board that ACTS's dual New York accreditations were invalid in New Jersey, and our accreditations were taken away. This move to eliminate rather than befriend would-be partners did not benefit the small school at all. ACTS died and so did the small Christian school very soon afterwards. At the same time, The Salvation Army's Newark Central Corps closed its buildings and decided to tear down Alaythia House. We visited the site a decade later to see nothing left but a used car lot occupying the site.

## Louisville, KY

Aída still felt a strong calling from the Lord to teach the New Testament, so we moved to Louisville, Kentucky, where she earned her PhD degree in New Testament at Southern Baptist Theological Seminary (her dissertation becoming her first book, the insightful *Paul's Literary Style*). I, who was already holding a secondary school certificate in English education from Rutgers, began teaching creative writing for the Jefferson County, Kentucky Board of Education's adult night school program and then was hired to teach for Sharon Darling's amazing, award-winning, pioneer Laubach Literacy program. After two years, Sharon appointed me her program's Teaching Coordinator for Jefferson County, and we set up and ran eight literacy and GED centers in the city of Louisville and its environs. I taught many adult students how to read and coached some of them through their GED high school-level equivalency degrees. For me, this fulfilled a gap I had noticed in my educational preparation, when I had found myself in Newark being able to teach storefront pastors to read the Greek New Testament but not able to navigate theology books, because of the difficulty of mastering English reading without proper preparation.

## Gordon-Conwell in Massachusetts

When Aída, at graduation, was invited to teach for Gordon-Conwell Theological Seminary (GCTS) in 1982, she and I, now with our young son Stephen, born in Kentucky, rented a truck and drove with all our belongings to Hamilton, Massachusetts. When Steve began school the next year and Aída was set teaching for GCTS, I began earning my ThD in systematic theology and ancient literature at Boston University School of Theology (BUSTh).

Shortly after I enrolled and began classes, I was invited to teach a class on prayer at GCTS in 1983 and was awarded my doctorate from BUSTh in 1986, the only ThD graduate that year (or, as I like to put it, I was both my class valedictorian and its bottom basement student!). Everyone else in my class was enjoying all the lectures and concerts and fellowship Boston University offered, but I had a small child at home. Our fabulous neighbors across the street, our town's chief dispatcher and police chief, Anne Marie and Walter (Butch) Cullen, with their own excellent son Sean, who was Steve's age, graciously welcomed Steve into their home each day I had class, which made traveling to Boston by train and subway doable. I could not have done the degree without them. Dad needed to be there when Mom had to teach and, with these saints' constant help, I was able to do it. God always supplies what we need to do God's will. I thank God for the Cullens adopting all of us as part of their vast and delightful family.

As for the Crohn's disease, it almost killed me from a complication that required the police to transport me one night for an emergency operation to nearby Beverly Hospital, done by a British Dr. House, who, with his team and God's grace, saved my life. I ended up staying about two and a half months in the hospital, but the team was able to cut out all my greatest damage from the years of this auto-immune condition and return me, by a resection, back to an early condition of the disease. My intestinal tract kept stopping and Hindu gastroenterologist Dr. M. Shah rescheduled an operation. I was reading Francis MacNutt's *The Power to Heal* and was intrigued by the prayer therapy idea, so I began to recruit people from the church and the hospital staff to pray for me so I would be treated to five prayers a day. My pastoral colleagues at Pilgrim Church, Paul Bricker, John Engle, and, of course, Aída, prayed for me daily in person or by telephone. One day, when I was in a severe amount of pain, Jeff Marks of *New England Concerts of Prayer* stopped in and, in his prayer, gathered all the pain under his hand and then began praying it away. He had to pick up his daughters so he had to leave before finishing. I told Aída what was happening and she picked right up where Jeff left off and prayed the rest of the pain away. As Spurgeon reports when he asked the Lord to take away a terrible bout with pain from his chronic condition of gout, a pain of this magnitude never reoccurred.[1] My intestines started again and Dr. Shah was so pleased that

1. Spurgeon et al., *C. H. Spurgeon Autobiography*, 197. For my fuller interaction with these moving memories of Pastor Spurgeon, please see Spencer and Spencer, *Joy Through the Night*, 166–69.

he canceled the second operation and said, "Let's put you on a therapy of prayer and prednisone," and that's what we did. Another of the miraculous results is that I was not supposed to be able to digest folic acid any longer, since my ileum was now gone, but God made that happen and I can still digest it today, even without the usual means to do so. During recovery, I wrote a chapter of my dissertation and even taught my seminary students in the hospital lounge the summer course I was scheduled to teach, while I was hooked up to two portable machines. One of the students, Evan Spencer (no direct relation to me, except being my brother in Jesus' family), brought the students over to class. I hate to waste time! That was my final hospitalization for Crohn's, although I still have a controlled remainder of this condition, which I treat with diet, rest, exercise, and Mesalamine.

As we were settling into Massachusetts, we had also made God some promises, to be fulfilled if we were allowed to stay. We had noticed that the area had no Reformed worship between Lynn and Newburyport (and the Lynn church was failing). The school had no journal. And the northeastern section of the *Evangelical Theological Society* had died out fifteen years prior. So, when GCTS asked Aída to stay and hired me to teach part-time, which was what my then-Crohn's-ravaged-health permitted, we planted Pilgrim Presbyterian Church with friends and students from the past, soon merging with an independent church, eventually becoming a union church. After a decade, Aída stepped down as volunteer pastor of organization, having led the church in the formation of its mission statement and its by-laws, staying active in the church but staying sensitive to balancing increasing school and child-rearing responsibilities; while I, still fathering and now teaching adjunctively, continued for thirty years as volunteer pastor of encouragement, preaching regularly, overseeing church discipline, Sunday school, praise music, and, for a decade, working in the courts with police prosecutors and court-appointed lawyers, helping to put addicts and lawbreakers into programs like The Salvation Army's Men's Social, as we used to call it, His Mansions, and Adult and Teen Challenge, with whom Pilgrim Church is still connected. Today, Pilgrim continues as an international church and is partnered with Gateway Presbyterian Church, a Kenyan church with whom it shares its building. Aída and I, now semi-retired, are honored as founding pastors and provide the worship music once a month, preaching and leading worship occasionally. The church is currently in good hands with the Rev. Valerie Crisman as pastor.

Aída and I also reestablished the *Evangelical Theological Society*'s (ETS) northeastern section, with Aída, who had chaired the southeastern region, now chairing this newly revived section for two years and I for the next two years. I also programmed all four of these initial years. When ETS asked our newly refurbished section to add New York, the northeastern section expanded outside of New England. For GCTS, Aída started its first ThM degree and a PhD support program with North-West University (NWU) in South Africa. Aída, and then I, both, eventually became external PhD supervisors for NWU, with whom we still work. I have had the privilege to serve as the external supervisor, with the excellent NWU supervisor and scholar Dr. Naas Ferreira, for the brilliant (now Dr.) Mark Shan, whose groundbreaking thesis on the Christian presence on China's Silk Road is correcting centuries-long errors. For GCTS, I established the Athanasius Teaching Scholars Program in theology and envisioned the *Africanus Journal*, which Aída and I founded together in conjunction with the GCTS Boston campus. For over forty years, we have been teaching and writing at Gordon-Conwell. As for Steve, after nine years serving as the night chef for 140 Gordon-Conwell students, he switched careers, going back to college to learn video production. Trading the preparation of food for the creation of films, he won many awards for his filmmaking from the local public access cable station, which then hired him as its director of production. And today, he is its director of programming for its news, announcement, and program stations.

What have I learned from all of this urban ministry? As I review each attempt we made to contribute our efforts to help each city in which we lived, working to do our small part in helping it become a kind of city of refuge, I realize the significance of Pss 46:1, 9:9, and 48:3, which extol God as our refuge and ever present help in combatting trouble. If God is being honored and our efforts are to promote the gospel, then, as our refuge and strength, the God of loaves and fishes multiplies these efforts and blends them with the work of others to bring about the reconciliation that God commands us to pursue. We do what we can, but it's not all up to us. It is simply our privilege to be allowed to make a small contribution expressing our gratitude for all God has done for us.

The Rev. Dr. William David Spencer is Distinguished Adjunct Professor of Theology and The Arts for Gordon Conwell Theological Seminary's Boston Campus/Center for Urban Ministerial Education (CUME). He has 335 publications at this writing, including articles, stories, poems, journalistic and editorial pieces, chapters in books by others, book and movie reviews, blog posts and other online publications, and eighteen books, this being the nineteenth. Two of his books, *Mysterium and Mystery: The Clerical Crime Novel* and *Chanting Down Babylon: The Rastafari Reader*, have been honored as definitive in their fields. He edited *Priscilla Papers* (*Christians for Biblical Equality International*) for ten years, and he and his wife, Gordon-Conwell senior professor of New Testament, the Rev. Dr. Aída Besançon Spencer, are cofounders of *Africanus Journal*, now in its eighteenth year. They are also cofounders of both the *House of Prisca and Aquila* series and *Africanus Monograph* series, as well as advisors for the *Urban Voice* series, for Wipf and Stock publishers. Bill has won twenty writing and editing awards. He has served in street ministry, college chaplaincy, prison ministry, church planting, and pastoring. In college and seminary, he led two evangelistic Jesus bands, playing coffee houses, colleges, festivals, churches, schools, and a prison across the eastern seaboard, and he also co-planted and co-led two evangelistic coffee houses. In 1973, he was ordained as a Presbyterian minister in a joint ordination service with his wife, who was also ordained. He has taught with New York Theological Seminary and a spin-off ministry to storefront churches, the Alpha-Omega Community Theological School (ACTS), helping develop a college-level theological program accredited by The King's College with four centers in Newark and Jersey City, NJ, and New York City. These were based in a Salvation Army Central Corps and three city churches. For four years in Louisville, Kentucky, he taught in Sharon Darling's Laubach Literacy program, eventually serving as teaching coordinator for Jefferson County, Kentucky, setting up and running eight adult literacy and GED high school equivalency classes for adults. Accompanying his wife, who was called to teach in Massachusetts, he helped plant and pastor Pilgrim Church, a storefront church in downtown Beverly, as volunteer pastor of encouragement for over thirty years, and he himself has served as a theology professor for forty-one years for Gordon-Conwell, having the blessing and delight to teach at its Boston campus since 1992. His trajectory in city ministering has stretched into sixty years and counting. He and his wife warmly invite you to join them on their blog *Applying Biblical Truths Today*.[2]

2. https://aandwspencer.blogspot.com.

Aída, Steve, and Bill Spencer in the Dominican Republic

# Conclusion

## Richard Bruce

Media consumption is America's number one activity. Sleep is number two. The same is probably true of the rest of the world. I used to ask students if this reflected their lives. One student said, "Yes, media consumption is number one, but what is this sleep you are talking about? What's that?" Media consumption consumes the majority of our waking hours. Over the course of a lifetime, media consumes several times the hours we spend working for money, dozens of times the hours we spend on education, over a hundred times the hours the average person spends in religious services, and perhaps more than a thousand times the hours the average person spends actually paying attention in religious services.[1]

Christians frequently say we need to bring the gospel message to where the people are. If so, we need to use the media because that is where people are. Writing is far from the only element in media, but it is an important part of media and, therefore, an important part of our Christian outreach.

Chapter 1 of *The Digital Evangelist: Expanding Your Ministry by Writing for Publication* features the advice of Rev. Dr. William David Spencer. He has published eighteen books, hundreds of articles, stories, poems, and has taught at Gordon-Conwell Theological Seminary for decades. The Spencers evangelize on digital media. In addition to these traditional ways of publishing and communicating, Rev. Dr. William David Spencer and Rev. Dr. Aída Besançon Spencer also maintain a blog, *Applying Biblical Truth*

1. I wrote this paragraph myself. I found the statistics that corresponded to mine in this article: Rodriguez, "Americans Are Now Spending."

*Today*,[2] and edit an academic journal with Gordon-Conwell Theological Seminary, *The Africanus Journal*,[3] which is also available online.

Some of William Spencer's advice you might have gotten from a secular writer, e.g., it is not just about pleasing yourself, you also must please editors and readers. But William Spencer adds another requirement: you must please God. William Spencer addresses publishing from a Christian perspective that the secular author would not. Some of Spencer's advice is for fiction. He has published short stories and novels. He advised us to use strong verbs and use actions to show character. One reason fiction can be important to Christian television ministry is that short stories and novels may be turned into movies and television series.

As a digital evangelist, I, myself, have a personal website explaining how to convince librarians to include Christian books into library collections. I think these web pages are an excellent way to expand my local ministry of convincing local librarians to include Christian books into my local public library (but no one is going to make these web pages into a movie or television series, at least I hope not).[4]

Most Christian writers may not create fiction, but those that do can have an important impact. William Spencer advised us to not start by trying to write a book. He suggests that we start with church newsletters, letters to the editor, local newspaper articles, and blog posts. Start projects you will actually finish. Spencer tells us that by doing short pieces we can list as completed and published, we can convince editors that you can finish longer projects. Jesus tells us in Luke 10:16, "Whoever can be trusted with very little can also be trusted with much, but whoever is dishonest with very little will also be dishonest with much." Editors use a similar principle. As writers, we build trust on small projects and work our way up to the book or, for most of us, just do the small projects. Spencer's advice that we write articles for local papers is excellent, even for those who do not intend to make writing a major part of their life. It is not really that hard to write a guest editorial, also called an op-ed piece, or even better still, a news article for a small local paper. This can give recent college graduates an effective way to convince potential employers that they can write, and furthermore, you can get a good bullet point on your resume with perhaps a day's work. It is better still if you can include a Christian message. For example, write

2. *Applying Biblical Truth Today*: https://aandwspencer.blogspot.com/.

3. *Africanus Journal*: https://www.gordonconwell.edu/cume/africanus-journal/.

4. "Personal Website of Richard Lee Bruce": https://richleebruce.com/.

about something that is happening at your church. I have done this several times myself, and it really is not that hard. For those who are serious about writing as a ministry, William Spencer advises writers to build a track record by publishing a lot. This is a summary of Dr. Spencer's chapter, which begins the book. "The Digital Evangelist" seminar that inspired this book included recommended reading: *The Cave of Little Faces*, *The Christian World Liberation Front*,[5] *Jesus Among the Homeless*.[6] Required reading for the seminar was the blog post "How My Journey to Jesus Teaches Me About Praying for the Middle East."[7]

In part 2 of this book, chapters 1 through 4 include writing by Jeanne C. DeFazio on the transformational impact of CWLF's Berkeley Street on her life; Julia C. Davis on the impact of her mother's faith on her own maturing faith, wisdom, views, and experiences as an African American Christian; Wilma Faye Mathis on *Jesus Among the Homeless*, her book about the ministry to the homeless in which she was involved; and Saideh H. Bonab on her blog post "How My Journey to Jesus Teaches Me About Praying for the Middle East."

Chapters 5 through 14 include the testimonies of notable Christians: Ted Baehr recounts how his life changed by reading the Bible; Susan Stafford reveals how her commitment to God eclipsed her successful media career; tough actor Mel Novak notes how his life was guided to Jesus by responding to his mother's powerful prayers; Bob Yerkes details how the Bible and a blind aunt's insights lifted this stuntman to spiritual heights; Gemma Wenger tells how her father's gentle faith enriched her life; Jozy Pollock explains how her hunger for God was satisfied; I, Richard Bruce, identified how I decided to convert to Catholicism; Terry McDermott shares how poetry can raise one's consciousness; Aaron Ezra Mann depicts how plays can awaken readers through the power of metaphorical drama; and Linda Lockhart counsels that testifying to our spiritual journeys may be the most powerful type of digital evangelism many Christians can do. In chapter 15, William David Spencer recalls his own life's journey as his living testimony to the guidance of God.

In conclusion, the Internet is a good place to share our poems, songs, pictures, and other creative efforts, particularly when they can help us spread the word of God. In Matt 9:37–38, Jesus mandates, "The harvest is

5. DeFazio, *Christian World Liberation Front*.

6. Mathis, *Jesus Among the Homeless*.

7. Bonab, "How My Journey to Jesus."

plentiful, but the laborers are few; therefore, pray earnestly to the Lord of the harvest to send out laborers into his harvest." Let us be those harvesters on the Internet.

# By the Same Authors

## Ted Baehr

*Behind the Scenes of the Golden Age of Hollywood and Broadway: The Legacy of Robert Allen*, coauthor with Richard E. Defay and C. C. Risenhoover.

*How to Succeed in Hollywood (Without Losing Your Soul): A Fieldguide for Christian Screenwriters, Actors, Producers, Directors, and More*, author.

*Getting the Word Out: How to Communicate the Gospel in Today's World*, author.

*The Christian Family Guide to Movies and Video*, author.

*Faith in God and Generals: An Anthology of Faith, Hope, and Love in the American Civil War*, author with contributions from Susan Wales.

*What Can We Watch Tonight?*, author.

*So You Want to Be in Pictures?*, author.

*The Media-Wise Family*, author.

*Narnia Beckons: C. S. Lewis's* The Lion, the Witch, and the Wardrobe *and Beyond*, author with contributions from James Baehr.

*The Amazing Grace of Freedom: The Inspiring Faith of William Wilberforce, the Slaves' Champion*, author with contributions from Ken and Susan Wales.

*The Culture-Wise Family*, author with contributions from Pat Boone.

*Frodo and Harry: Understanding Visual Media and Its Impact on Our Lives*, coauthor with Tom Snyder.

*Redeeming the Screens: Living Stories of Media "Ministers" Bringing the Message of Jesus Christ to the Entertainment Industry*, contributing author.

## Saideh H. Bonab

"How My Journey to Jesus Teaches Me About Praying for the Middle East," coauthor with Jeanne DeFazio in *Applying Biblical Truths Today*.

*Upon Seeing God And His Glory He Was Ready To Go*, author.

## Richard Bruce

"It Was in the Cards," in *Catholic Digest*, author.

"A Possible Solution to the Vouchers Issue" in *New Oxford Review*, author.

## Julia C. Davis

*Empowering English Language Learners: Successful Strategies of Christian Educators*, contributing author.

*Specialist Fourth Class John Joseph DeFazio: Advocating for Disabled American Veterans*, contributing author.

*An Artistic Tribute to Harriet Tubman*, coeditor with Jeanne C DeFazio

*The Commission: The God Who Calls Us to Be a Voice During a Pandemic, Wild Fires, and Racial Violence*, contributing author.

*Finding a Better Way*, contributing author.

*The Christian World Liberation Front: The Jesus Movement's Model of Renewal and Reform for the Postmodern World.*

*Jesus Among the Homeless: Successful Strategies of Christian Ministers to the Marginalized*, contributing author.

*Otto and the White Dove*, contributing author.

*Letting Go*, contributing author.

*The Journey Home*, contributing author.

*Media Fellowship International: A Model Christian Outreach to the Entertainment Industry*, contributing author.

## Jeanne C. DeFazio

*Creative Ways to Build Christian Community*, coeditor with John P. Lathrop.

*How to Have an Attitude of Gratitude on the Night Shift*, coauthor with Teresa Flowers.

*Redeeming the Screens: Living Stories of Media "Ministers" Bringing the Message of Jesus Christ to the Entertainment Industry*, coeditor with William David Spencer.

*Berkeley Street Theatre: How Improvisation and Street Theater Emerged as Christian Outreach to the Culture of the Time*, editor.

*Empowering English Language Learners: Successful Strategies of Christian Educators*, coeditor with William David Spencer.

*Keeping the Dream Alive: A Reflection on the Art of Harriet Lorence Nesbitt*, author.

*Specialist Fourth Class John Joseph DeFazio: Advocating for Disabled American Veterans*, editor.

*Christian Egalitarian Leadership: Empowering the Whole Church According to the Scriptures*, contributing author.

*An Artistic Tribute to Harriet Tubman*, coeditor with Julia C Davis.

*The Commission: The God Who Calls Us to Be a Voice During a Pandemic, Wild Fires, and Racial Violence*, editor.

*Finding a Better Way*, editor.

*The Christian World Liberation Front: The Jesus Movement's Model of Renewal and Reform for the Postmodern World*, editor.

*Jesus Among the Homeless: Successful Strategies of Christian Ministers to the Marginalized*, contributing author.

*Otto and the White Dove*, editor.

*Letting Go*, coauthor with Terry McDermott.

*The Journey Home*, editor.

*Media Fellowship International: A Model Christian Outreach to the Entertainment Industry*, coeditor with Susan G. Stafford.

## Linda Lockhart

*Jesus Among the Homeless: Successful Strategies of Christian Ministers to the Marginalized*, contributing author.

*Finding a Better Way*, contributing author.

*The Journey Home*, contributing author.

*The Commission: The God Who Calls Us to Be a Voice During a Pandemic, Wild Fires, and Racial Violence*, contributing author.

## Aaron Ezra Mann

### Screenplays

*One Day in the Park*

*Java Time*

*The Squirrels*

*Deadliest Island*

*Horsing Around*

*Big Cat*

*Fast People*

*Little Darlin*

### Books

*Otto and the White Dove*, author.

*Jesus Among the Homeless: Successful Strategies of Christian Ministers to the Marginalized*, contributing author.

*The Commission: The God Who Calls Us to Be a Voice During a Pandemic, Wild Fires, and Racial Violence*, contributing author.

*Finding a Better Way*, contributing author.

*The Journey Home*, contributing author.

*Media Fellowship International: A Model Christian Outreach to the Entertainment Industry*, contributing author.

## Wilma Faye Mathis

*An Artistic Tribute to Harriet Tubman*, contributing author.

*The Commission: The God Who Calls Us to Be a Voice During a Pandemic, Wild Fires, and Racial Violence*, contributing author.

*Finding a Better Way*, contributing author.

*When Women Speak*, contributing author.

*Black Girl Cry*, contributing author.

*God's Masterpiece*, author.

*Jesus Among the Homeless: Successful Strategies of Christian Ministers to the Marginalized*, author.

*The Journey Home*, contributing author

## Terry McDermott

### Poems

The Crimson Wall

The Day Before Tomorrow

A Child's Lament

Never Said Goodbye

A Smile Sadder Than Tears

The Fifth Vote

Grace Alone

A Prayer for All Mothers

Color Me Dead

Death Roe

The American Lie

Blood on a Shoe

I Am an American

A Song Never Sung

Through the Eyes of Jesus

Double Cross

Many Tears Ago

If Only I Had Known

### Books

*Otto and the White Dove*, contributing author.

*Letting Go*, coauthor with Jeanne C DeFazio.

*The Journey Home*, contributing author.

*Media Fellowship International: A Model Christian Outreach to the Entertainment Industry*, contributing author.

## Mel Novak

*Redeeming the Screens: Living Stories of Media "Ministers" Bringing the Message of Jesus Christ to the Entertainment Industry*, contributing author.

*Jesus Among the Homeless: Successful Strategies of Christian Ministers to the Marginalized*, contributing author.

*The Commission: The God Who Calls Us to Be a Voice During a Pandemic, Wild Fires, and Racial Violence*, contributing author.

*The Journey Home*, contributing author.

## Jozy Pollock

*Redeeming the Screens: Living Stories of Media "Ministers" Bringing the Message of Jesus Christ to the Entertainment Industry*, contributing author.

*Jesus Among the Homeless: Successful Strategies of Christian Ministers to the Marginalized*, contributing author.

*The Commission: The God Who Calls Us to Be a Voice During a Pandemic, Wild Fires, and Racial Violence*, contributing author.

*Finding a Better Way*, contributing author.

*The Journey Home*, contributing author.

*Backstage Pass to Heaven*, author.

## William David Spencer

*Cave of Little Faces: A Novel of Adventure on the Haitian Border*, coauthor with Aída Besançon Spencer.

*Chanting Down Babylon: The Rastafari Reader*, coeditor with Nathaniel Samuel Murrell and Adrian Anthony McFarlane.

*Christian Egalitarian Leadership: Empowering the Whole Church According to the Scriptures*, edited with Aída Besançon Spencer.

*Dread Jesus: Views of Jesus in Rastafari*, author.

*Empowering English Language Learners: Successful Strategies of Christian Educators*, edited with Jeanne C. DeFazio.

*The Global God, Evangelical Multicultural Views of God*, coeditor with Aída Besançon Spencer.

*Global Voices on Biblical Equality: Women and Men Ministering Together in the Church*, coeditor with Aída Besançon Spencer and Mimi Haddad.

*God Through the Looking Glass, Glimpses from the Arts*, coeditor with Aída Besançon Spencer.

*The Goddess Revival: A Biblical Response to Goddess Spirituality*, coauthor with Aída Besançon Spencer, Catherine Clark Kroeger, Donna F. G. Hailson.

*Joy Through the Night: Biblical Resources on Suffering*, coauthor with Aída Besançon Spencer.

*Marriage at the Crossroads: Couples in Conversation About Discipleship, Gender Roles, Decision Making, and Intimacy*, coauthor with Aída Besançon Spencer, Steven R. Tracy, and Celestia G. Tracy.

*Mysterium and Mystery: The Clerical Crime Novel*, author.

*Name in the Papers: An Inner-City Adventure Novel*, author.

*The Prayer Life of Jesus, Shout of Agony: Revelation of Love, a Commentary*, coauthor with Aída Besançon Spencer.

*Reaching for the New Jerusalem: A Biblical and Theological Framework for the City*, coeditor with Seong Park and Aída Besançon Spencer.

*Redeeming the Screens: Living Stories of Media "Ministers" Bringing the Message of Jesus Christ to the Entertainment Industry*, coeditor with Jeanne C. DeFazio.

*Second Corinthians: Bible Study Commentary*, coauthor with Aída Besançon Spencer.

*Three in One: Analogies for the Trinity*, author.

## Susan Stafford

*Redeeming the Screens: Living Stories of Media "Ministers" Bringing the Message of Jesus Christ to the Entertainment Industry*, contributing author.

*The Commission: The God Who Calls Us to Be a Voice During a Pandemic, Wild Fires, and Racial Violence*, contributing author.

*The Journey Home*, contributing author.

*Media Fellowship International: A Model Outreach to the Entertainment Industry*, coeditor with Jeanne C DeFazio.

*Stop the Wheel, I Want to Get Off*, author.

## Gemma Wenger

*Redeeming the Screens: Living Stories of Media "Ministers" Bringing the Message of Jesus Christ to the Entertainment Industry*, contributing author.

*Empowering English Language Learners: Successful Strategies of Christian Educators*, contributing author.

*The Commission: The God Who Calls Us to Be a Voice During a Pandemic, Wild Fires, and Racial Violence*, contributing author.

*Finding a Better Way*, contributing author.

*Jesus Among the Homeless: Successful Strategies of Christian Ministers to the Marginalized*, contributing author.

*Media Fellowship International: A Model Outreach to the Entertainment Industry*, contributing author.

*The Journey Home*, contributing author.

*Creative Ways to Build Christianity*, contributing author.

*Christian Egalitarian Leadership: Empowering the Whole Community According to the Scriptures*, contributing author.

## Bob Yerkes

*Redeeming the Screens: Living Stories of Media "Ministers" Bringing the Message of Jesus Christ to the Entertainment Industry*, contributing author.

*The Commission: The God Who Calls Us to Be a Voice During a Pandemic, Wild Fires, and Racial Violence*, contributing author.

*The Journey Home*, contributing author.

*Media Fellowship International: A Model Outreach to the Entertainment Industry*, contributing author.

*Creative Ways to Build Christianity*, contributing author.

# Bibliography


A., Christine. "The Influence of Social Media on Christian Faith and Devotion." Medium, Oct. 3, 2023. https://medium.com/@csajourney/the-influence-of-social-media-on-christian-faith-and-devotion-5f12e7c71e2b.

Almquist, Curtis. "Making Meaning." *Cowley* 47.1 (2020) 10–15. https://issuu.com/ssje/docs/2020_cowley_fall___pages.

Azumah, John. *My Neighbour's Faith: Islam Explained for Muslims.* Nairobi: Word Alive, 2020.

Bonab, Saideh, with Jeanne DeFazio. "How My Journey to Jesus Teaches Me About Praying for the Middle East." *Applying Biblical Truths Today* (blog), June 9, 2025. https://aandwspencer.blogspot.com/2025/06/how-my-journey-to-jesus-teaches-me.html.

Boud, David. "What Is Peer Learning and Why Is It Important?" *Rakan ELIT PPD Kulai* (blog), July 4, 2014. https://sipsisckulaijaya.wordpress.com/2014/07/04/what-is-peer-learning-and-why-is-it-important/.

Bruce, Richard. "It Was in the Cards." *Catholic Digest* 57.3 (1993) 34. https://richleebruce.com/digest.html.

———. "Possible Solution to the Vouchers Issue." *New Oxford Review*, Jan. 2002.

Burge, Ryan P. "Fifty Years After MLK, Sunday Segregation Isn't Theological." *Christianity Today*, Apr. 4, 2018. https://www.christianitytoday.com/2018/04/50-years-mlk-black-white-evangelicals-segregated-sunday-gss/.

Chesterton, G. K. "The Lawlessness of Lawyers." In *The Uses of Diversity*. London: Methuen, 1920.

Dahlburg, John-Thor. "A Stricken Man's Tale of Triumph." *Boston Sunday Globe*, Mar. 16, 1997.

Davis, Julia C., and Jeanne DeFazio, eds. *An Artistic Tribute to Harriet Tubman.* Eugene, OR: Resource, 2021.

———."The Alternative Jesus: Psychedelic Christ." *Time*, June 21, 1971. https://time.com/archive/6839039/the-alternative-jesus-psychedelic-christ/.

DeFazio, Jeanne C. *Berkeley Street Theatre: How Improvisation and Street Theater Emerged as a Christian Outreach to the Culture of the Time.* House of Prisca and Aquila. Eugene, OR: Wipf & Stock, 2017.

———. *The Christian World Liberation Front: The Jesus Movement's Model of Revival and Social Reform for the Postmodern Church.* House of Prisca and Aquila. Eugene, OR: Wipf & Stock, 2022.

———, ed. *The Commission: The God Who Calls Us to Be a Voice During a Pandemic, Wildfires, and Racial Violence.* Eugene, OR: Wipf & Stock, 2021.

———. "The Digital Evangelist: Expanding Your Ministry by Writing for Publication." Sept. 25, 2025. YouTube video, 1:13:13. https://www.youtube.com/watch?v=eHHb079VdJQ.

———. *Finding A Better Way*. Eugene, OR: Wipf & Stock, 2021.

———. *The Journey Home*. Eugene, OR: Resource, 2024.

DeFazio, Jeanne C., and John Lathrop, eds. *Creative Ways to Build Christian Community*. House of Prisca and Aquila. Eugene, OR: Wipf & Stock, 2013.

DeFazio, Jeanne C., and Susan G. Stafford. eds. *Media Fellowship International: A Model Christian Outreach to the Entertainment Industry*. Eugene, OR: Resource, 2025.

DeFazio, Jeanne C., and William David Spencer, eds. *Empowering English Language Learners: Successful Strategies of Christian Educators*. House of Prisca and Aquila. Eugene, OR: Wipf & Stock, 2018.

———, eds. *Redeeming the Screens*. House of Prisca and Aquila. Eugene, OR: Wipf & Stock, 2016.

Everett, Burgess. "Senators Duel Over 'Race Card.'" Politico, May 22, 2014. https://www.politico.com/story/2014/05/jay-rockefeller-john-johnson-race-106983.

Flowers, Teresa, and Jeanne DeFazio. *How to Have an Attitude of Gratitude on the Night Shift*. Eugene, OR: Resource, 2014.

Holton, DeLaynie. "'I Had Told You I Did Not Print': Poems Published in Dickinson's Lifetime." Emily Dickinson Museum, 2023. https://www.emilydickinsonmuseum.org/publishedinlifetime/.

*House of Prisca and Aquila*. "About Us." https://sites.google.com/site/houseofpriscaandaquila/about-us.

Jackman, Steph. "Short Attention Spans and Long-Term Retention: The Evolution of Learning in the Digital Space." IACET, May 30, 2024. https://www.iacet.org/events/iacet-blog/blog-articles/short-attention-spans-and-long-term-retention-the-evolution-of-learning-in-the-digital-space/.

Janzer, Anne. "The (Not Really) Shrinking Reader Attention Span." https://annejanzer.com>shrinking-reader-attention-span.

Littleton, Jeanette Gardner. "How Much Can I Quote? A Guideline for Writers and Editors." *Liaison*, summer 2018. https://www.evangelicalpress.com/how-much-can-i-quote-a-guideline-for-writers-and-editors/.

Lockhart, Linda. "Review of *An Artistic Tribute to Harriet Tubman*." *Africanus Journal* 15.2 (2023) 46.

Mann, Ezra. *Otto and the White Dove*. Eugene, OR: Resource, 2023.

Mathis, Wilma Faye. *Jesus Among the Homeless: Successful Strategies of Christian Ministers to the Marginalized*. House of Prisca and Aquila. Eugene, OR: Wipf & Stock, 2023.

NBC Palm Springs. "Study Reveals Declining Attention Spans in the Digital Age." Sept. 10, 2025. https://www.nbcpalmsprings.com/therogginreport/2025/09/10/study-reveals-declining-attention-spans-in-the-digital-age.

Pruitt, Shane. "5 Ways to Use Social Media to Share the Gospel." North American Mission Board, Feb. 28, 2023. https://www.namb.net/resource/5-ways-to-use-social-media-to-share-the-gospel/

Rodriguez, Ashley. "Americans Are Now Spending Eleven Hours Each Day Consuming Media." Quartz, July 20, 2022. https://qz.com/1344501/americans-now-spend-11-hours-with-media-in-an-average-day-study.

Rogers, James. *The Dictionary of Clichés*. New York: Random House, 1983.

Rosenwald, Michael S. "Bob Yerkes, Bruised but Durable Hollywood Stuntman, Dies at 92." *New York Times*, Oct. 17, 2024. https://www.nytimes.com/2024/10/17/movies/bob-yerkes-dead.html.

Sabloff, Gabriel, dir. *Dancer and the Dame*. Dancer and the Dame, www.PureFlix.com/DancerAndTheDame.

Schrad, Lisa. "What Difference Does Prayer Make in the World?" *InterVarsity* (blog), Oct. 13, 2017. https://intervarsity.org/blog/what-difference-does-prayer-make-world.

Seech, Zachary. *Logic in Everyday Life: Practical Reasoning Skills*. Belmont, CA: Wadsworth, 1988.

Spencer, Aida Besançon, and William David Spencer, eds. *Christian Egalitarian Leadership: Empowering the Whole Church According to the Scriptures*. House of Prisca and Aquila. Eugene, OR: Wipf & Stock, 2020.

———. *Joy Through the Night: Biblical Resources on Suffering*. Eugene, OR: Wipf & Stock, 2007.

Spurgeon, C. H., et al. *C. H. Spurgeon Autobiography 2: The Full Harvest 1860–1892*. Edinburgh: Banner of Truth Trust, 1973.

Stack Exchange. "What's the Origin of the Idiom 'On the Same Page'?" https://english.stackexchange.com/questions/117519/whats-the-origin-of-the-idiom-on-the-same-page.

Stobbe, Les. *The Making of a Writer and Publisher*. Winter Springs, FL: EABooks, 2021.

Taogaga, Karen. "On Faith Alone Jozy Pollock Story." Feb. 25, 2010. YouTube video, 7:07. https://www.youtube.com/watch?v=auNvGVfes5U.

Webster's Unabridged Dictionary. "Publication." New York: Random House, 1987.

WikiChristian. "Jozy Pollock." https://wikichristian.org/wiki/en/Jozy_Pollock.

Wikipedia. "Bob Yerkes." https://en.wikipedia.org/wiki/Bob_Yerkes.

———. "Gemma Wenger." https://en.wikipedia.org/wiki/Gemma_Wenger.

———. "Mel Novak." https://en.wikipedia.org/wiki/Mel_Novak.

———. "Susan Stafford." https://en.wikipedia.org/wiki/Susan_Stafford.

———. "Ted Baehr." https://en.wikipedia.org/wiki/Ted_Baehr.

Wipf and Stock Publishers. "Author Guide: Version 10.0 (October 2025)." https://dhjhkxawhe8q4.cloudfront.net/wipf-and-stock-v2-wp/wp-content/uploads/2025/10/23182731/WS_AuthorGuide_10.pdf.

World Health Organization. "Malnutrition Rates Reach Alarming Levels in Gaza, WHO warns." July 27, 2025. https://www.who.int/news/item/27-07-2025-malnutrition-rates-reach-alarming-levels-in-gaza—who-warns.

www.ingramcontent.com/pod-product-compliance
Lightning Source LLC
LaVergne TN
LVHW020632100826
845148LV00012B/2156